Roses in December

THE AUTOBIOGRAPHY OF
ERNEST MARSHALL
HOWSE

Ernest Marshall Howse

With a foreword by
CLAUDE T. BISSELL

WOOD LAKE BOOKS
Winfield, BC
V0H 2C0

Cover Design and Layout: James Taylor

ISBN   0-919599-07-9

Canadian Cataloguing in Publication Data

Howse, Ernest Marshall, 1902-
    Roses in December

    ISBN 0-919599-07-9

    1. Howse, Ernest Marshall, 1902-
2. United Church of Canada - Clergy -
Biography. 3. Clergy - Canada - Biography.
I. Title.
BX9883.H68A37 287'.92'0924 C82-091366-9

First Printing, October, 1982
Second Printing, December, 1982
Third Printing, November 1983

Printed in Canada by
Friesen Printers
Altona, Manitoba
R0G 0B0

DEDICATED
in gratitude
and hope
to

MARGERY
DAVID
GEORGE

KATHY
SCOTT

ANDREW
JENNIFER

and all
in their line

CONTENTS

An Introduction:

Ernest Howse is one of the great Canadian preachers of our time. Although he grew up in a deeply Methodist environment with its delight in a fervent, evangelical style, he was more attracted to the scholarly tradition that he encountered at Pine Hill Divinity College, formerly a Presbyterian Divinity College. He was not, however, given to abstruse theological speculation, and he was never seduced by the fashionable jargon of the contemporary secular priests. He is certainly a scholarly preacher—when a young man he had written a doctoral dissertation that became an important book for the understanding of nineteenth century English social history—and he continued throughout his life to be both preacher and author. But the scholarship emerges unobtrusively, presented with lucidity and wit.

One of the fascinations of this biography is the contrast between the life of the mature man, who occupied major pulpits in Canada and the United States, and the life of the youth who grew up in a Newfoundland that was a tenuous network of small fishing communities, clinging to a rocky coastline—on one side a desolate wilderness, and on the other, the vast and turbulent ocean. The account of the Newfoundland years is lovely social history, full of revealing detail, suffused with love of the austere land, of its warmhearted people, and, in particular, of his family that never permitted the rigours of daily living to obscure the primacy of mind and spirit.

Ernest Howse is a pastor who inspires respect and devotion. He is also an unapologetic spokesman for great (and often unpopular) causes. Two causes are dear to him: the elimination of racial and religious bigotry; and the search for an ideal world community devoted to peace and sustained by a common faith. He is a tough-minded liberal for whom ideas are a prologue to action, and faith the fruit of mental struggle.

In early 1979, Ernest Howse, aged seventy-seven, looked and acted like a man in the full vigour of life. Then, a routine medical check-up revealed what was diagnosed as an advanced cancer. He had at the most, he was told, only six months to live. He confronted this final crisis with resolution and faith; his reflections at the time were contained in the last newspaper column he wrote and that is reproduced in this book. But now, aged eighty, after three operations and extended treatments, he speaks and acts with his old vivacity and enthusiasm. His words for Easter Sunday, 1979, ring out today more confidently than ever: "Whenever it may be that I hear for the last time the last syllable of 'The Lord God omnipotent reigneth' I will know that what that exultant Hallelujah is saying about life will be more than all the rest of recorded speech can explain about death."

Claude T. Bissell

Foreword:

"Now start talking."

So spoke my elder son David as he placed on my study desk that modern temptation to loquacity, a tape recorder.

Ever since I retired, my three children had been urging me—while I still remained presumably sane, and certainly at large—to set down in writing some recollections of life back in those different and peculiar days of my childhood in Newfoundland, recalling an order of life and circumstance now vanished into the limbo of the past.

Despite their urging, I had never gotten around to writing. I probably never would have, but for the tape recorder. One day I picked up the microphone, and without plan or structure afore-thought, I started talking. In the following days, as memory turned the scroll, I spoke the record.

At that time my intent went no further than to transcribe the tapes into typescript and have a few photocopies made for the family. By then, by the kind of fortuitous occurrence that has characterized my life, James Taylor of Wood Lake Books somehow heard of what I was doing, and asked if I could prepare the material for publica-tion.

That was a different kettle of fish. Talking is not writing. I had to begin the tedious task of recasting, from beginning to end, in my clumsy one finger pattern, every paragraph I had spoken so easily in-to the mike.

The reader should know, then, that this book is in no sense a springboard for a theological treatise. It is not an *Apologia pro Vita Sua* nor an outpouring of guilt-filled confessions. It is merely an at-tempt to bring back a "remembrance of things past"; to recreate and preserve for generations beyond my own some picture of the life and times of the eight decades of the 20th Century.

In the macrocosm of the years the tale of one life is only a microcosm. But in some ways, the large can be understood only in the little. The memories stored as part of a single human life may evoke other memories—in turn rich threads in the strange and fascinating tapestry of human life and aspiration.

Here then is a kaleidoscope of recollections, a fraction only from the long experience of eighty years, in which in faint minor key I may say like Caesar: "... all of which I saw, and part of which I was."

Ernest Marshall Howse

God gave us memory

that we might have

roses in December.

J.M. Barrie

The Very Rev. Ernest Marshall Howse, S.T.M., Ph.D., D.Litt., D.D.
Moderator of the United Church of Canada
1964-1966

Chapter 1

Before My Time

*the origins of my family
in Newfoundland's
rugged outports*

Newfoundland is the oldest settled part of the New World. Water Street in St. John's is the oldest street in the Western Hemisphere. People have been tramping the coastline of St. John's harbour since 1498, the year after Newfoundland's discovery by John Cabot.

This is not to say anything about the people who may have been there centuries earlier; the Vikings, the Irish and others.

Before Newfoundland joined Canada, the French in Quebec were the earliest Canadian settlers; but Quebec clearly comes second to Newfoundland. In 1583, twenty-five years before Champlain brought his first settlers to Quebec, Sir Humphrey Gilbert, on the authority of Queen Elizabeth, established in Newfoundland the first overseas British colony. At that time, he reported that he found St. John's already a populous and important place. The beginning of habitation in St. John's had come half a century earlier. In a letter dated August 3, 1527, a sea captain, John Rut, wrote about finding eleven ships from Normandy, one from Brittany, and two from Portugal in the port of St. John's. By 1540, vessels from London, Bristol and other ports were making St. John's their habitual harbour. In 1615, more than a quarter of a century before Maisonneuve founded Montreal, another English official, Sir Richard Whitbourne, set up in Newfoundland the first court of justice in the New World.

Yet despite early beginnings, settlement in Newfoundland grew only in spasms and with glacial slowness. The vessels that came annually to fish in Newfoundland waters were sent out by English fishing firms which did not want any interference or competition from a fishing industry based in Newfoundland itself. So, for a long time, the captain of an English vessel was forbidden to leave in

The desolate shores of Goosebery Island, and the site where my grandfather James Howse built his house.

Newfoundland any of his crew or passengers. Until well into the 18th century, the English parliament appointed the Captain of the first English vessel which sailed that spring into St. John's harbour to be the yearly governor of Newfoundland.

Not until 1729 did Parliament appoint a permanent Governor.

The legacy of this form of government was that many of the early settlements of Newfoundland were in effect beyond the law and, hence, records of these times are scanty and incomplete. To compound this defect, the capital city, St. John's, was destroyed three times by fire, and each time precious records were irretrievably lost.

It is not surprising that I find myself today in the predicament of many other Newfoundlanders whose family tree goes far into Newfoundland's past. When in recent years I became curious to know the lineage of the Howse family in Newfoundland, I found that I came to an abrupt stop in the latter part of the 18th century.

I found the oldest records not in parish registers, of which few survive, but in mouldering and partly indecipherable tombstones in the ancient graveyard of Gooseberry Island, about ten miles off the coast of Bonavista Bay on Newfoundland's northeast shore.

Gooseberry Island, so-called, is in strict description two islands. That up-thrust of the earth's crust is split by a tickle (channel) from one hundred to two hundred yards wide and about three-quarters of a mile long. That tickle forms a sheltering harbour; my family surely needed it, for on the outer side of that rugged reef the vast Atlantic stretches unbroken to Ireland.

Who came first to settle on that lonely scrap of rock is unknown. But it was a good fishing base. In the latter part of the 19th century it was home for a community of about fifty families. Sixteen were Howses. Today it is again vacant, but the old graveyard and its weathering stones remain.

I have never been on Gooseberry Island, never seen those slabs of stone, their terse inscriptions bringing lone voices from the past. But my brother Claude has carefully examined and photographed them, and through many years has gathered as much information as he could by talking with survivors of my father's generation.

The oldest stone of all goes back to my father's great-grandfather John Howse. Unfortunately, that was a slab of sandstone; though the name and some of the inscription is still clear, the date is obliterated. We can infer that it was about 1790. Then comes a son, also John (but with the variation that on his tombstone the name is spelt House). He was born in 1797 and died 24 years later, leaving four sons, one of whom, James Howse, was my grandfather. James died in 1876 when my father was twelve. My father was born in 1864—a full century before I, his eldest son, was elected in Newfoundland as Moderator of the United Church of Canada.

The Howses, at least those in our direct family lineage, were not only fishermen; they were shipbuilders. The vessels that they sailed to Labrador, they themselves built on Gooseberry Island.

Almost anyone can build a house. What you have to do mainly is

My FATHERS
NANE WAS
CHARLES
EmH

*The tombstone,
on Gooseberry Island,
of Catherine Feltham Howse,
my grandmother.*

to saw pieces of board to the right length and nail them together. But to build a schooner for the Labrador fishery or the trans-Atlantic trade, to fashion her hull so that she will handle well in heavy storms, will neither ship waves at the stern nor plunge at the bow, and will not roll too much in broadside waves—that calls for craftsmanship of a high order, craftsmanship acquired only through generations of survival.

One other chore requiring hard labour was the cutting and the fashioning of the "knees," as they were called. Knees are the roughly right-angled connections that join the beams of the vessel to the ribs. They serve the same purpose as those little right-angled pieces of metal that we can now buy at a hardware store to reinforce a shelf, or perhaps the legs of a chair. Usually they were made from the roots of trees and then shaped with an adze for precise fitting.

Today I stand in awe, as I think of the sheer amount of hard work, the hours of slugging toil that it took from the time the fisherman put his axe over his shoulder and went into the woods to cut down the first tree, to the time when the schooner was sailing out of the harbour, built and furnished with all the complex accoutrements essential for a sailing vessel heading out for hundreds of miles to Northern Labrador—or perhaps across the Atlantic to Portugal or

A pit saw, of the kind the Howse brothers used to cut the planks for their schooner, Orange Lily.
This saw was still in use in La Scie when I went there to teach.

down to Barbados or Jamaica.

The shipbuilder first carved a model of the hull, skillfully fashioning every curve so that the ship would handle at sea as he designed it to handle. From that little model he would create a schooner matching his design, down to its slightest curve. The skill required, shaping the ribs with such finesse that each separate plank going from stem to stern would touch each rib exactly, awakens a great respect for those craftsmen of former days.

My father and his brothers, in their primitive little shipyard on Gooseberry Island, built the schooner named the *Orange Lily,* in which for many years they fished on the Labrador. They built the vessel from lumber that they themselves had sawed—by muscle power. They got their masts from pine trees still available at a few accessible places along the coast. The planks for the hull, they got by cutting down suitable trees on the mainland, shipping them across to the island and then making them into lumber with their own pit saw. A pit saw, so-called, was a long saw with two handles. Usually it was not in a pit but rather in a raised frame as in a service bay for automobiles today. One man standing on top and one below, they would saw the logs lengthways.

My father and his brothers built their schooner in two years of such time as they could steal from their regular occupations. They did it so well that not only did the *Orange Lily* survive a generation of North Atlantic storms, but once my father skippered the vessel from Gooseberry Island to St. John's in six hours, said to be a record yet unequalled for sailing vessels.

My father, at the time of the launching of the *Orange Lily*, was just nineteen years of age. That summer he skippered the vessel to the Labrador. But he had first gone to Labrador as a hand at the age of twelve, the year his father died. In his first years he was shipped on as a half shareman, but at age fourteen he shipped as a full shareman—that is as a man. At nineteen he was a veteran.

No wonder people spoke of wooden ships and iron men.

One final word: When the battered *Orange Lily* came to the end of her long and valiant career, the next generation of the Howse family—including a nephew of my father, the Rev. Gilbert Howse, at the time of this writing bright and alert in his nineties at Albright Manor, Beamsville, Ontario—built another schooner which sailed to the Labrador for another generation.

And that, to the best of my knowledge, was the last schooner to be built on Gooseberry Island.

As to my mother's family, records are more available, though in places patchy, for a grim reason. When my mother was five years old, her mother and a number of neighbors and kin were wiped out by that scourge of the past, an epidemic of diptheria.

Thereafter my mother, then Elfrida Palmer, was brought up by her sister, Catherine Pelley. Both our grandmothers were also named Catherine: father's, Catherine Feltham; mother's Catherine Tilly. The name is now commonly spelt Tilley; but my mother's grandfather, John Tilly, signed his name the shorter way, and so set the pattern for his family.

John Tilly, my great-great-grandfather, was a remarkable man. He is reputed to have taught himself to read at age twenty-six, and then to have bought a Greek New Testament and taught himself Greek, and read Homer's *Iliad*. Apparently he wrote poetry; but only a fragment of a long poem, written in his almost indecipherable hand, is now preserved in the Newfoundland archives.

He became a justice of the peace, and a man of substance. He owned a large farm and a sawmill, and he introduced into Newfoundland both the brick-making industry and the tinning of salmon.

During my mother's childhood the Pelleys and the Palmers lived in the little village of George's Brook, or in nearby Shoal Harbour, on the shores of a deep inlet in Trinity Bay. Mrs. Charles Pelley, my mother's sister, was nineteen years older than mother, and had married at age sixteen—a normal age for the time. She lived into her nineties, in her last years with only one leg. She could never become reconciled to the fact that even after her leg was cut off, she could still feel it aching, but could no longer put her foot in a pan of hot water. In our house she was always referred to just as Auntie.

If the Tillys and the Pelleys produced remarkable individuals generation after generation, my mother's father, David Palmer, added to our ancestry one more who was, in the British term, a "character."

After diptheria had taken his first wife, mother's mother, he married again. His second wife died and he married again. His third wife died and he married once more. In a reception to celebrate his fourth wedding he responded to a congratulatory speech (the Methodist equivalent of a toast) with this comforting reflection: "God has been good to me. He has seen fit to give me three wives, and to take them from me. Now he has given me a fourth, and if he

those who read few books
did read
the Bible

sees fit to take her I am sure he will have another to take her place.''

The bride's reflection is not recorded.

The Palmers broadened our family heritage; for David's father was Israel Palmer, a Jewish peddlar (packman was the Newfoundland word) who settled in the George's Brook area in the early 1800's. Later he owned and operated a sawmill, and his son David followed in the same business. If my memory is correct, my mother told me that her grandmother (Israel's wife) was a French girl. There were still many Newfoundlanders of French origin.

Altogether our family lineage was richly mixed. It is too bad that so little has been done to preserve the record of former days, in some ways so meagre; in others so full.

A century ago when my father and mother were growing up in outport Newfoundland, the literate were an elite. The sea captains, the merchants, the clergy, the school-teachers had prestige and influence. Their education may often have been narrow; but many of the pupils of those one or two-roomed schools had this asset—what they did know, they knew well. They had been drilled in the three Rs. They had been taught grammar. They could keep books, or ship's logs. They knew the parts of speech, and they could properly use their mother tongue. In some ways they may have been better grounded in the essentials of education than many of our high-school graduates today.

Among converted Methodists, at least, even those who read few other books did read the Bible. Their minds were enlarged by its scope, and their speech fashioned by its phrases.

I remember my father's speaking with admiration about a parishioner in the Blackhead circuit. That simple fisherman was, said my father, one of the most eloquent men he had ever heard. His speech was leavened by the language of the King James Bible. Unconsciously he clothed his thought in the stately, vivid diction of the book which was his lifetime companion.

Both my father and my mother fitted themselves first to be school teachers. Their children lived in a literate atmosphere. This may partly explain why, despite the meagre finances of a parsonage, of the six children who grew up in their household, five earned university degrees and the sixth an R.N. (Registered Nurse) diploma.

I recall that when I went to my first pastoral charge as a student probationer, my mother gave me her Webster's Unabridged Dictionary, that she had had since her teaching days before I was born. She thought that with a Bible and a dictionary I had two books essential for a minister.

at twenty-two his whole life was changed in a Methodist revival

My father grew up with little regular schooling. But since at age 19 he was able to skipper a schooner, he must have learned to read and write and do arithmetic. And that no doubt, was all that then seemed necessary for a full and useful life.

But at age twenty-two his whole life was suddenly changed. He was converted in a Methodist revival.

The Methodists were then vital and active in Newfoundland. My father's family, and indeed most other Newfoundlanders, belonged to the Anglican church—except those in the Irish sections, where all were Roman Catholic.

After his conversion my father felt the call to go into the ministry. His brothers supported him loyally, and made it possible for him to begin his studies. So he left the close-knit little Howse community on Gooseberry Island and went first to St. John's to the Methodist College—an institution which later my mother also attended to prepare her for teaching. The so-called college was really a boarding school with curriculum up to about the present high school level. (In due course not only our parents but all six of their children spent at least one year in that institution.)

When my father had finished the courses available there, he spent some years as a schoolmaster to save money for further education.

When he had sufficient money to make the venture (in those days it did not require much) he left Newfoundland, and went to Mt. Allison University in Sackville, N.B., and on to further studies at Garrett Biblical Institute, Chicago. With his theological diploma from that institution, he went back to Newfoundland, and lived there the rest of his life.

18

Newfoundland was not then, as it is now, a province of Canada. Like Canada itself it was a British Dominion; but no more a part of Canada than it was of Australia. It was not till 1949 that, as the Newfoundlanders sometimes put it, Newfoundland took Canada into Confederation.

My mother at times had a wistful longing to move the family to Canada. There, she thought, her children would have a better chance. My father, however, thought that Newfoundland, among his own people, was where he was called to minister.

I think father was right. The common people in Newfoundland towns and villages had nothing in the range of their lives that he did not know and understand. If some schooner were overdue in those vast seas, my father knew as well as anyone could what were the hazards and chances, the fears and hopes. In those rough days, when every fishing village and almost every family was somewhere scarred by tragedy, my father stood with the most stricken of his parishioners, knowing their feelings and sharing their sorrow. In a way not possible to an outsider, he was one of them. He was of the essence of Newfoundland.

In the end, my father's concern for his call proved stronger than my mother's concern for the success of her numerous brood. Both Mother and Father took it for granted that, wherever we were, all six of us were destined to dazzle and guide the next generation.

The first three children: left to right,
Millicent, Kathleen, and me, all dressed in the latest fashions.
I

Chapter 2:

Stirrings of Life

*my family
and my heritage*

The place to which the Methodist Church sent my father to begin his ministry was Tilt Cove, a mining town at the northwest corner of Notre Dame Bay.

More than a quarter of a century later I was to know Tilt Cove quite well. I went to La Scie, a few miles farther north, to begin my first job as school teacher. But by then the copper had petered out. Tilt Cove was only a hamlet of fishermen, with memories of a better past. Some of them still remembered my father with surprising affection. Obviously he had been a great pastor. But I know nothing of my father's Tilt Cove days. I was not born until—in the itinerant fashion of the Methodist—he had moved to another ministry elsewhere.

Tilt Cove days, however, marked the birth of two of our family. The first, a girl, unfortunately died at birth. The next, also a girl, was named Millicent. She was to be for forty years a missionary of the United Church in Angola, Africa.

When father left Tilt Cove, he moved across Notre Dame Bay to Twillingate. Twillingate was an island; but that did not make much difference; most settlements in Newfoundland were accessible only by water. There were few roads anywhere linking one village to another. Indeed, when I went to Twillingate in 1965 on a Moderatorial tour, even then the only way to get an automobile to Twillingate was by an ancient ferry. Since then a causeway has been built.

My parents had not been long in Twillingate when I arrived, in 1902. Some fourteen months later another girl, Kathleen, brought the family to five. Like others in the family she began teaching before she was out of her teens. Later she came to Toronto to study

21

*my sister and I
held in their arms
while the storm raged on*

nursing at the General Hospital. After getting her R.N. she practised her profession in Toronto for many years. The parsonage in which Kathleen and I were born was still in good condition when, sixty years later, I went back to Twillingate as Moderator.

When we left Twillingate I was just coming to my third birthday. So my recollections are vague. Yet somehow I preserved three childhood memories.

The first was that of a horse's hooves beating their peculiar music as we crossed a bridge, I suppose over some little inlet of the sea.

The second was of two men running across a field and jumping over a barrel laid sideways across an opening where a gate should have been—I suppose to keep the sheep or the goats in or out.

The third was of red canvas in the kitchen.

Red canvas in the kitchen was a trademark of Newfoundland. I can remember in later days putting on the red paint myself. The floor covering would be canvas taken from discarded sails that still had good spots in them. It would be nailed down wall-to-wall over the wooden floor, and painted red. Why red I don't know, unless it was the brightest of all possible colors. Certainly the Twillingate red—perhaps a new coat of paint—made its impression on my mind, even at three years of age.

Following Twillingate, my father's next pastorate was Burin. Burin is on a peninsula jutting out from the south coast of Newfoundland; to get there we had to go by coastal steamer almost half-way around the island's rugged coast. But the Methodists, when they moved their clergy, never seemed to consider geography.

As with Twillingate, I remember Burin only in incidentals. I still have in my mind a vague picture of a winding street—little more than a gravel path—which went by our house and wound its way up to the little church on the hill. To me though, the church did not seem little but big.

I remember a bad thunderstorm. We had friends in the house—it was probably too stormy for them to go home by boat. I remember how my sisters and I (as yet I had no brothers) were held in the arms

22

of the older folk while the storm raged on.

I remember one of our servant girls, Dorcas. She stayed with us for several years and was like one of the family. When her sweetheart wanted to see her, he would walk down the lane behind our house, and at the appropriate moment burst into song. Unfortunately he sang in a strident monotone; and the only song he knew was a then popular evangelical hymn, "Come, Great Deliverer, Come."

I remember going out in a boat with my father to see a dead whale. Before being towed ashore to be cut up, it was anchored, floating with its white belly above the water. I was impressed with the corrugated pattern of the white belly.

I remember something else, though at the time I had no idea how important it was. I remember going out with my father in something new—a boat that did not need any oars. It had an engine. As we raced around the harbour—probably making up to three miles an hour—I was much impressed with the putt-putt that marked the magic of this new thing.

That first motor engine was the same kind that I myself used in later years, a heavy one-cylinder affair, perhaps running on kerosene oil, and perhaps not even having a spark plug, but only a primitive make-and-break. It would have a large propeller, and, for a fishing boat thirty feet long, might be three horse power. It would not move the boat fast, but somewhat faster than such a heavy boat could be rowed. And it was a lot easier on those who would otherwise be using the oars.

Years after that first motorboat ride, the centuries-old picture of the trapskiff was still common: four men, each with a long home-made oar out the side, a fifth man sculling and steering with another oar out the stern.

But inexorably the oars went, and the engines came. In all the years my father was fishing he never saw a motor-boat; he still was at the oars. But that morning in Burin Harbour, my father and I without knowing it, saw the passing of what had been, and the prophecy of what was to come.

Burin brought my parents both joy and sorrow. Shortly after they arrived came the birth of another girl, whom they christened Edna Louise. Alas! When she was slightly over two years of age she was stricken with a malady the doctor could not diagnose. After drawn-out suffering she died. I remember the funeral; I remember her grave in the churchyard on the hill, and the little headstone.

Before Edna's death the family had welcomed its second boy, Claude. He became a government geologist for Newfoundland, and directed much of the prospecting which led to the discovery of the great iron ore deposits in Labrador. With the one little airplane he could have in the Depression, he led an exciting and hazardous life with some hairbreadth escapes from death. Later he joined the Iron Ore Company of Canada and remained their consultant until he retired. He probably knew more about that vast Labrador terrain than any other man in the world.

In Burin I first went to school, but I remember little about it. My childhood memories really begin with our next circuit—Blackhead.

Spring

*a boy's world
in a Methodist parsonage*

My memories of Blackhead begin at Carbonear, 12 miles away. Waiting there was a welcoming contingent of Blackhead parishioners. A cortege of horses and carriages was lined up to take the minister and his family in proud procession on that last twelve mile lap.

The carriage in which I was taken had a fold-up seat, something like those found long afterwards in seven-passenger automobiles. On that seat, I had my back to the horse, a position I didn't like. Nevertheless, at seven years of age, I had never before been in such a magnificent vehicle. I was a proud boy.

With a flurry of introductions and everyone in high spirits, we started off for Blackhead. There the church women in immemorial fashion had prepared a bountiful reception; and there we began what were in some ways, for both my father and our family, the best years of our lives.

Blackhead was a fishing village at the centre of a three point charge. Nearby, at Harbour Grace, was the birthplace of Methodism in North America, when the Rev. Laurence Coughlin preached the first Methodist sermon outside the British Isles. Soon after, he converted almost 100 percent of the Blackhead population.

Two or three miles south was a smaller village, Broad Cove; and two or three miles north was a still smaller village, Adams Cove. My father had to preach at all three places each Sunday, normally at Blackhead in the evening—for the evening service was then the most important service of the day.

In a Methodist village in those days, not only were the church and the minister, in a way almost unimaginable now, the centre of the whole community life; but the church service was the most important event of the week.

In my mind's eye, I can still see a familiar Sunday evening scene as the road through Blackhead became a moving stream of men, women and children on their way to church. I remember especially how those people could sing. They would shake the building as they belted out the old Methodist hymns with their rollicking tunes. Nowhere in the world was that prayer, "For those in peril on the sea," sung with more emotional fervour than in churches like that at Blackhead.

The minister had not only the duties of an evangelist. He often was the key figure in the whole range of community life.

In particular, a Newfoundland minister had one responsibility which made him different from his brethren in Canada, or the United States, or perhaps than anywhere else in the world. His place in the commumity cannot be understood without understanding the Newfoundland system of education.

Newfoundland then had no public schools and has none today, though the minister's place in the process has been shifted substantially to laymen. Newfoundland schools were run by churches. Each year the government would give a per capita grant to the churches, mainly the Roman Catholics, the Anglicans and the Methodists.

With this money, and what the various churches raised by fees or otherwise, the denominations operated their own schools. My father and many other Methodists did not like this system. Some Anglicans, too, were against it, but of course it was exactly as the Roman Catholics wished. And so, with some changes, it remains to this day.

In practice, the system was better than might be expected because many Newfoundland communities were composed almost entirely of one denomination. Blackhead, for example, was almost 100 percent Methodist. Another community might be as strongly Anglican (or Church of England as the name was then). Roman Catholics lived mainly in Roman Catholic villages in their own sections of the island.

Whatever the faults or merits of this system, the consequence was that the clergy in effect ran the schools. The Methodist minister normally became the chairman of the local school boards.

When, for example, at age 18, I became the Methodist probationer in the remote village of Burgeo, I also became the instant chairman of the school board.

The complete family, at the swing in our garden at Blackhead:
front row, Father, Carl, Bill, Claude, Mother;
back row, Kathleen, E.M.H. and Millicent.

I hope that it will not now be regarded as too flagrant nepotism if I add that when the teacher of Burgeo's senior students became sick, I sent for my sister Kathleen, then 18 and out of work, and had her take the position for the school year.

As I said, the Newfoundland system was not all bad.

Responsibility for the schools added greatly to my father's work in Blackhead. Early in his pastorate he took two bold steps. He started to build a new and larger church in Broad Cove, and a new and larger school in Blackhead.

As minister he was in charge of everything. The primary task was to raise the money. Fortunately this burden was lightened by the fact that much of the labour was free. Most fishermen were boat builders and skilled carpenters, and in off season they would gather to work on the church project. Many of them, including my father, were quite competent to do the whole job.

In my first school year at Blackhead, I went to the old building that had served for generations. It was a dingy place with long desks and benches on either side of a centre aisle.

a number of
stinging whacks
on the open palm

The new building had two rooms. They were bright and spacious with large windows and gleaming hardwood floors. The heat was still supplied by wood-burning stoves, inherently disposed to be too hot or too cold. And the toilet facilities were still a shack in the corner of the school grounds—one building divided, with two holes each for boys and girls. But now even that building was new—and painted! Everything was up-to-date in the Blackhead school room.

As for the old row desks, marred by generations of irrepressible schoolboys carving initials or otherwise making their mark in the world, they had been replaced by others modern as could be. Each desk seated only two pupils, and was fastened to the floor so that it could not be shoved around by ill-behaved pupils.

As I think back, however, I cannot believe that any pupil would dare cause too much trouble. The master had in his desk a convenient piece of rubber belting (the current improvement on the old-time leather strap). And he did not believe in sparing the rod and spoiling the child. He did not interrupt his classes for discipline, but if he saw something which he thought merited punishment he would just call the name of the culprit. The boy (I do not remember a girl) would then come up and stand till the class was over. Then the miscreant would be summoned to receive the just reward for his deeds—a number of stinging whacks on the open palm. All the others would watch with curiosity to see how valiantly he would stand the ordeal.

I must admit that I was at times the recipient of that caning. I presume that I must attribute to that stimulating experience the development of whatever excellencies I later attained. You might say that I learned to warm both hands before the fire of life.

Seriously, I must add that I liked our Blackhead schoolmaster (I did not like all my teachers everywhere) and held him in great respect. If I had met him at any time in later days I would have counted it a privilege. The ill effects of a caning can be greatly overestimated.

All in all, our life in Blackhead comes back to me in a golden haze of memory.

By modern standards we might well have been classed as poor. Certainly we had little money. A Methodist minister then had a nominal salary of $900 a year. But there were bad years (though probably not at Blackhead) when the salary received was less. Once, the total my father received was $750. Even in good years most of the salary may have been received in erratic sums when the fish was sold in the fall. My mother told me that she had times when she could not lay her hands on a five-cent piece. I warrant, though, that somehow before Sunday she managed to get a penny apiece for the children to put in the collection plate. For the minister's children to be without their offering would have been a disgrace.

Whatever we lacked in cash, nowhere did I have a sense of poverty. Frugality was a way of life, but we lacked nothing. On the contrary I always had the feeling that we were the well-to-do. This may have been in part because we were always helping others, compared with whom we were rich. In those days, when welfare was not even a concept, a fishing village always had widows desperately trying to raise their children without a breadwinner in the family. For them the chief source of help was the church. Even as children we knew what real poverty was; we were fittingly reminded to "count our blessings." We lived with a sense of having plenty.

We always had plenty of food, and we did not think it strange that after Christmas we were not likely to see any oranges till the next Christmas. We always had warm clothing, our thick socks and mitts knit and then darned by mother. And we had our Sunday best.

We always had a servant girl in lieu of washing machines and other modern conveniences. In Blackhead we also had a man to look after the horse, and provide general help. The girl's pay was five dollars a month; and girls were often eager to get a place in the parsonage and so a better chance to learn to keep house.

We lived in a parsonage that was by village standards large and imposing. It was 80 years old when we were there and destined to last many years thereafter. We could and did keep a spare room not only for friends but also for the travelling dignitaries of the church. Many of the names that I saw in our church literature became live people to me.

We had a barn where we kept our hens, our cow (for one period two cows) and our horse. So we produced our own eggs and our own milk. In the spring, the cow would calve and after a proper time we would kill the calf for veal. When we decided to get rid of the second cow, mother thought that we should ask ten cents a pound for the beef that we sold; but father thought that we ought not to appear greedy and should ask only nine cents.

As an extra, whenever we killed an animal, its skin provided us with a warm mat for the floor of our unheated bedrooms.

The "horse" in which we had the most pride was a fine trotting mare, Nell. We had a carriage for the summer, and for the winter a sleigh. The more fashionable had a "cutter." What we, like many others had, was an ordinary sled of the kind used for hauling wood. We put a wide plank from front to back so that passengers sat sideways with their feet on the running board, while the driver, to get a good view, sat on a box at the rear. It was style enough for us.

Because we had a horse, I learned to ride. I did not know at the time how useful that was to be later on the Saskatchewan prairies.

Unfortunately Nell got colic with some complications, and died. In those days, the problem of disposal was not difficult. We hauled her on a cart to an isolated section of the coast and tipped her over a cliff into the sea. In due course the processes of nature would take care of everything.

On parsonage property we had three fields, including a pasture with a running brook (where we once found an old cannon ball, a relic of the days when the French were marauding the land). We also had a vegetable garden. We grew our own potatoes and turnips and cabbage and carrots, bounteous quantities of which we stored in our root cellar in the large, partially unfloored basement.

In all this our pattern of life was similar to that of our parishioners. In the early days of the century a Newfoundland fishing village was a remarkably self-sufficient community. Historically it had an unusual economic order. For example, there were no property or land taxes. Every Newfoundland family, even the poorest, had its own untaxed house. And the houses built by the owners, with the help of their friends, were all two stories to provide bedrooms for the large families then normal. Along with the house was the inevitable garden. Families grew their own vegetables, and, besides chickens, usually kept a pig.

That was why in the thirties, when the Great Depression came to Newfoundland, the public relief allotment was *seven cents per person per day!* The theory was that if people were out of work, or if they could not sell their fish, at least they could fish for themselves and they could grow their own food. The seven cents were for a few

the world had not found a more delicious treat

necessities: tea, flour, molasses.

In Blackhead, we bought most of the necessities in bulk. Until World War I, I never saw flour sold in anything smaller than a 196 pound barrel. The sugar barrel was bigger, 300 pounds. The general store would break that into smaller lots, though the idea of buying a pound or two would seem as silly as buying a pound or two of potatoes. (Incidentally, so far as I remember, potatoes were never sold in stores any more than fish were. Anyone who bought potatoes bought a surplus barrel from a neighbour.)

Molasses was a great supplement to sugar. It came in huge casks called puncheons, made of heavy staves. When the puncheons were empty they were sawed in two and used as "puncheon tubs" for washing fish.

To sell the molasses, the store keeper would lay the puncheon on its side in a heavy frame, put a spigot in the head, and from there draw off the molasses. Most people would bring small kegs and buy perhaps ten to twenty gallons at a time.

We kept a molasses keg at the parsonage. One of the real treats we children enjoyed after coming home from school was having bread covered with both butter and molasses. *That* was luxury. Sometimes it even seemed extravagance.

When the molasses puncheon was empty, the storekeeper would set it upright, and then loosen the top hoop and take out the head. What had been the bottom side would have a sediment of perhaps three or four inches of molasses sugar. That served a variety of purposes but none more delightful than letting small boys dip their hands into it and come up with a big gob of gooey molasses sugar. We thought that the world had not found a more delicious treat.

One other favorite edible, especially for an outdoors "mug-up" (in modern vocabulary, a snack) was what we called hardtack. Sea biscuit is a better known name. This was made from flour and looked something like a roll, and was as hard as a piece of board, but brittle so that it could be eaten. It had one advantage; it would not

a schooner
might limp home
as much as a month late

freeze. It was edible where a sandwich would be frozen solid. Also it could last indefinitely; and it was used, of course, for making brewis.

Fish and brewis was to Newfoundlanders what haggis was to Scotsmen. It was made from soaked and cooked hardtack supplemented with fish and garnished with "scruntions"—that is, little squares of fat pork browned in the frying pan and poured liberally over the brewis. I remember fish and brewis with scruntions as a delicious breakfast on a Sunday morning. On ordinary days we had porridge, usually with molasses instead of sugar. I liked it better. This was not the fancy molasses that supermarkets now sell in small cartons, but old fashioned Caribbean black-strap that really had body.

Turning from food—which at times does become advisable—I recall the blacksmith shop. Every fall it became the busiest place in town and a great centre for passing gossip. Blackhead, a prosperous community, had a number of Newfoundland ponies. The Newfoundland dog is well known but the Newfoundland pony also has its place as a distinctive breed. It is small, say 600-700 pounds, has short legs and is not much good for trotting but can do quite well with a gallop. And for its size it is amazingly strong.

To understand how we looked after our cows or sheep and our horses, in that bygone Newfoundland, one must understand that normal habitation was just a fringe of small communities settled by the shores of that giver of life, the sea. To move inland a few miles, sometimes a few yards, was to be in the woods. In this wild land everyone could go to get firewood, or let their cattle roam at will.

Fishermen's ponies were rarely needed until after the fishing was over. So in summer they were simply turned loose. Sometimes, in the Fall, it was quite a job to find a wandering pony, but nearly always the stray was rounded up and put back in his stall.

Before being set free for the summer the ponies were all unshod. So when they were rounded up, a lot of ponies had to line up at the blacksmith's. To watch the blacksmith at his job was quite an experience.

The blacksmith would begin with unfinished shoes, heat them red-hot, shape them to the horse's hoof, burn them to a perfect fit, nail them on and then with a sharp knife and a big rasp finish the job as neat as could be. Sometimes, if the pony were being shod for the first time, that blacksmith had quite a fight on his hands. But he always came off victor, and we always enjoyed the fun.

No remembrance of things past in the Newfoundland, when both the twentieth century and I were young, can escape the fact that the nexus linking every aspect of Newfoundland life was the humble codfish.

Curiously, Newfoundlanders seldom gave tongue to that word, codfish. Salmon, herring, haddock, capelin and any number of other species they called by name; but for codfish they needed no name—a codfish was simply a fish. A boatload of herring was herring; but a boatload of cod was fish.

I had no direct participation in that branch of the fishery in which my father had spent his early years, the yearly odyssey by schooner to the Labrador. I never saw Labrador till long years later when I first saw it from the air, and still later landed there by plane. But I remember the bright glory of spring when in a single day I could see perhaps one hundred and fifty vessels sailing northward, their white canvas dotting the blue sea. In the fall they hoped to return laden down to what they called "one strake above water"; that is to say, the width of one plank as freeboard. But starting off they rode high, though they carried as unseen freight the hopes and fears of hundreds of families left behind.

On those schooners, before radio was dreamed of, communication was limited to the range of the human eye. When a ship passed beyond the horizon into the seas that stretch two thousand miles between the continents, the crew were cut off from all contact with their families, and the families from all knowledge of the men who were gone.

At times when the fleet was returning in the autumn, an unfortunate ship might be caught by a storm and driven half way across the Atlantic. As the other ships made port, anxiety centred on the one missing. At times a schooner battered by successive gales might limp home, perhaps minus a mast, as much as a month late. That interval of waiting was an agony that aged wives even when it did not make widows. And on Sunday evenings the congregation would have one heart as it sang once more, "For those in peril on the sea."

The other main branch of the cod fishery was the shore fishery. This was carried on at conveninet locations near the shores of each little village. Much of this home fishing was with traps—essentially large boxes of netting anchored to the sea bottom and kept upright by cork floats. (Glass floats came later.)

Despite the portent for the future I had seen in that motor-boat in Burin, while we were at Blackhead, the age-old pattern of four men rowing and the fifth steering with a sculling oar out the stern was still the only available method of locomotion. Not until after the First World War did the motorboat become the norm.

As I grew older, I went on occasion in the boat of a neighbour to haul a trap, and shared the excitement as we dragged that net up from the bottom and dumped the day's catch of fish into our trap-skiff.

Fish meant codfish. We threw aside as worthless other species now habitually used for food. Indeed in Newfoundland, we were indifferent to a great variety of available sea food. For example, we never ate flounders—flatfish, we called them. That may have been because flatfish tended to gather wherever sewage ran into the sea.

the grave was shallow, the odor overpowering

We never ate clams; we dug them for bait; and before they were used they were often a stinking mess. We used to dismiss even haddock as a low priced second grade fish. And we never thought of condescending to squid; we probably would have chosen to eat our sea boots first.

Besides "fish," herring and salmon were Newfoundland favourites. They were caught not in a trap but in gill nets, and were sold both for local consumption and for export. When the salmon began to run they sold as high as ten cents a pound, but in time they would drop to five cents.

In any case, the price of fish had little concern for the minister. Parishioners would no more think of charging the minister for a fish than for a drink of water. I am not sure, however, that the easy generosity of pre-war Blackhead continued through all father's later pastorates.

One other item about memories of fish. No one who has seen the sight can forget an annual Newfoundland spectacular: the arrival of

34

that extraordinary little fish, the capelin.

Capelin are small, about six inches long and narrow in girth. Either fresh or salted and dried they are delicious—in my opinion better than kippered herring. In our Blackhead days, and later, we always had some dried capelin among the winter stores.

Capelin used to appear each year approximately in early June, remain for two or three weeks and then disappear. The Russians have now found, far away in the Atlantic, the home grounds from which they come. But in Newfoundland, in my boyhood, all we knew was that the capelin came like buds in the springtime.

They came in stupendous, almost incomprehensible, numbers. When the schools moved in to the shore they seemed to cover acres. They were caught mainly by dropping a seine around a sizable pocket of them and dipping them up by the boatload. Where there were beaches, it was possible simply to back a cart to the sea and scoop up the capelin with a dipnet.

On a fine summer day when the sun was shining and the waves were rolling in on the beach, the capelin were an extraordinary sight. Every wave would throw them up on the shore in their silvery millions, wriggling and shining as they rolled back with the receding sea.

Only tiny fractions of the great capelin schools were caught and only portions of these were used for food. Many were used for fertilizer. At that time, there was no commercial fertilizer; and many people did not have cows or horses to provide manure. So they would dig shallow trenches between the rows of their potatoes or other vegetables, throw on the capelin, and scrape back the earth.

Alas! The fishy grave was sometimes too shallow, and when the half-covered capelin were half decomposed, the odor coming from the gardens was overpowering. For all the glory of their arrival, the capelin left nothing more unforgettable than that final smell.

Many other Blackhead memories remain, like gates open to tempting fields as yet unentered. But the full chronicles of that past time would run to volumes. So they must be left, a fleeting record in the fleshy tablets of memory.

That is the nature of human existence. Life in Blackhead remains reality while I and others are alive to recall it; but when our memories are no more, part of what we saw and much of what we were, will be gone forever. Every human being takes to eternity some small part of time.

One essential record of our Blackhead life I must not omit. Our family kept on growing. We came to Blackhead with four children, and we left with six. The two newcomers were boys, first Carl, and then Bill.

During World War II, Bill, who had by then graduated from Dalhousie University in Marine Biology, volunteered for service in the Canadian Air Force. In October 1942, he was travelling to Newfoundland by sea because weather conditions made air flight unavailable. He was on the passenger steamer *Cariboo*, within sight of the home shore, when it was sunk by a German submarine.

Bill was among the missing.

The tragedy was the more poignant because he was returning to Carbonear to the home which he and his brothers had built for our parents after father retired. He was coming home to be married; the wedding was arranged for the day after he was to land. The wedding flowers were already in the parsonage the morning the torpedo struck.

It was the first break in our family since the death in Burin of little Edna. My mother lived her remaining days under the shadow of that dreadful sorrow.

Carl, also a graduate of Dalhousie University, also volunteered for service in the Canadian Air Force. Part of the time he was on the Newfoundland East Coast where our planes were hunting German submarines. More ships than the public then knew of were sunk in those waters.

Following the war, Carl returned to high school teaching in Ontario. In his later years he spent a long term as principal of a high school in Odessa on the fringes of Kingston, Ontario.

At the time of this writing, Carl, Claude and I are the only survivors of the six children who made up our family in Blackhead.

Chapter 3:

Branching Out

school days
in Bonavista

In 1913, my father moved from Blackhead to Bonavista. Bonavista was larger than any of our previous places of residence. It had a population of 4000 with roughly equal communities of Methodist and Church of England, and a sizable minority that was Roman Catholic.

Cape Bonavista, a few miles from the town, was a long peninsula jutting out into the Atlantic. That promontory was the first land sighted by John Cabot on his voyage of discovery in 1497. The word which became Bonavista was Cabot's exclamation in his own Portuguese tongue, "O happy sight!" Other mariners since then have greeted that cape with different sentiments. Its rough headland breaks the swell of the North Atlantic sweeping across 2000 miles of stormy sea. The adjacent coastline is steep and dangerous, and Bonavista itself has but a poor harbour.

Our parsonage was back a few hundred feet from the shore, but I can remember after a heavy gale having to wash our windows to clear the salt left by the flying spray.

Cape Bonavista has one of the oldest lighthouses on the Atlantic coast. It stands almost at the brow of a precipice dropping sheer to the sea. The elevation, if I remember rightly, is 104 feet. Once when I was taking a visiting clergyman from Toronto to see the historic sight, the lighthouse keeper told us that during an extraordinary storm in the early 20th century, a monstrous wave completely engulfed that cape, broke in the door of the lighthouse, rolled across the floor and then broke open another door.

To stand on Cape Bonavista on a calm day, to look down at the surf far below, and to think of a wave massive enough to break over

what a devastating
feeling it is
to be lost

that cliff, is to stagger the imagination.

I have never seen Cape Bonavista in such a storm. But there and elsewhere, I have seen some dreadful storms. I recall one Bonavista gale of almost cyclonic fury, in which, in a single day, I think, 53 boats and three schooners sank in the harbour itself and along the shore.

I have no doubt that most of the wrecks could be rescued and repaired. But a storm like that makes one think of the Breton fishermen's prayer: "O God! Our boats are so small and thy ocean so vast."

We went to Bonavista just after the building of a new parsonage. It had cost a tremendous sum—over $4,000. It had an imposing veranda, with gingerbread carving and large rooms inside. It overlooked a river, running into the sea. In front of the parsonage, the river broadened into a small lake—which we called a pond. A spur railway line ran across part of the pond. There I once saw a derailed locomotive run off the trestle and plunge into the water.

Between the parsonage and the pond were two fields: one a pasture, the other a vegetable garden and a hayfield. In Bonavista, we did not keep a horse. The circuit was limited to the town and the minister could reach all his parishioners on foot. We did keep chickens and a cow. We had, indeed, a purebred Jersey, called Gwen. Gwen was a remarkable producer of milk, and once brought us first prize at the Bonavista Agricultural Exhibition. That was fame!

In view of my maturity—I was then ten years of age—my parents judged me old enough to look after Gwen. I had to get up about six o'clock to milk her before breakfast, clean out the stable and start her off into the woods for her free pasture. After school I had to go to the woods to find her, drive her home and milk her again.

Once when I was looking for Gwen, she happened to have wandered beyond her usual haunts. It was in the fall when darkness comes early. As I kept going farther looking for the lost cow and listening for the bell she always wore, I got lost myself. I suddenly became aware that I could not see any familiar landmark, and that I did not know which way was home.

After some hurried exploration, I did hear that familiar cowbell, and did judge the right way to head for home. I arrived after nightfall, just as Father was setting out to look for me.

I learned at that time what a devastating feeling it is to be lost. On a couple of occasions later, I have been for a while, alone and lost; never long enough to be in serious danger, but long enough to be in anxious uncertainty. Perhaps to lose our bearings, to be uncertain of the right way to go, ("I don't know what is right or wrong any more") is a shattering experience in realms other than geographical.

Our school days in Bonavista were much the same as in other towns and places. School was a single building with two rooms, one, the primary, taught by a young woman, and the upper school taught by a man. In Bonavista it was a yearly succession of men.

Except perhaps for one year with a red-headed young man named Smith, no teacher of distinction marked our time. One master who held the post there for one year before he moved on—by request—was an old man, coming to the end of his career, and very crotchety. The pupils gave him a hard time. He happened to require a cushion wherever he sat, and twice during the year the cushion was stolen by miscreants whose identity was not an unbroken secret, but of whom the entire upper room professed themselves to be totally unaware.

A similar misfortune befell the leather strap which the master kept in a locked desk. The lock was never broken, but during the year a succession of three leather straps evaporated.

Even in those days, school was more than the academic curriculum. One of the extra-curricular activities was the "Concert" put on by the pupils, directed by the lady teacher, the minister's wife, or whatever other competent person could be impressed from the community.

A feature in the concert would be recitations. Young performers would declaim supposedly humorous or perhaps touching poems—something like "The Wreck of the Hesperus," or perhaps "Little Boy Blue," or even some rolling prose such as Pitt's Reply to Walpole.

The recitation, like the solo for the musically gifted, was an item in which for a moment one could become a star. It was in these recitations that I first began to speak to an audience.

Much earlier in Blackhead, when I was perhaps seven or eight years old, I had begun imitating my father by organizing church services in the kitchen, or the barn, or even outdoors—any place when I could gather some of my younger siblings and their playmates. I cannot recall what I used to preach about. But even then audience tolerance never reached permission for me to sing a solo.

All else in Bonavista fades in significance with the coming of World War I in 1914. In the beginning, that trouble in Europe seemed a long way from us. We had no presentiment that we were to be involved in a struggle which would change human life, even in Newfoundland. For the most part the people of Newfoundland, except those living in the Irish localities, were of English descent. They were keenly aware of their roots in the Old Country and intensely loyal. As the war dragged on, it intruded more and more into the lives of ordinary folk, especially when Britain's need for men became desperate and the recruiting campaigns for Army and Navy (no Air Force yet) stepped up in intensity.

We began to have large public meetings to recruit volunteers. In church hall or fraternal lodge, leading figures of Newfoundland life would tell outport crowds what was happening in France, or Belgium, or on the high seas, and how grave and perilous the issues were. All this would lead to the climax, the intense appeal to young men to answer the call of their country.

These recruiting meetings were the most emotional appeals these loyal progeny of England had ever heard—apart perhaps from some great religious revival. And the young men of Newfoundland responded to a degree unsurpassed by any other part of the British Empire.

It needs to be understood that World War I came with emotions far different from those of World War II. I remember both wars. In the first, many young men considered it a duty, an honour, and almost a privilege to fight for their King and country. These young men had never known anything about war; and neither, for the most part, had their parents. To enlist was considered a great adventure. Many volunteers lied about their age so that they could get away to war and the glory of heroes.

I myself, though inwardly scared, thought that to give one's life to the cause of right was a noble deed, and I was anxious to go. But the war ended just as I was coming up sixteen. So I was a little too young for World War I, just as later I was a little too old (and myopic) for

the war intruded more and more into lives of ordinary folk

World War II. At the time it was a disappointment: I see now that I was fortunate.

Thinking of both wars, I can see how different was the emotional response of many who went to World War II. They were not thinking of adventure and glory. They did not want to go. They knew that it was a repulsive business. But, facing Hitler and fascism, they felt that they had no alternative.

Again I shared the feeling of the time. When in the desperate days of 1940 I knew that I could not be accepted for regular service in army, navy or air force, I still felt I should do something. So even with two children, and a third shortly to be born, I wrote a letter to the Governor General of Canada saying that if there were any special tasks in which I might serve, I would be glad to do so.

I received a letter of thanks; but I was never called, and so it was that I skirted the two world wars, missing both.

In Bonavista, during World War I, we did not have TV or radio. We could have gotten a St. John's paper no more than a day late. Up to that time we had never, as I remember, taken a daily newspaper. Neither had many other families in any Newfoundland outport.

What every community did have was a telegraph office. That was our marvellous link with the outer world. The telegraph operator used to put a page of typewritten news in a glass-fronted notice board outside the door. That bulletin brought the first tidings of everything, including all the changing fortunes of the war.

My father would often send me to read the bulletin and bring back the news. He expected that I would be able to come back and recite to him that latest sheet, the paragraphs starting: "London message says..., Dispatch from Paris confirms...," and so on.

I was put on my mettle to see whether I could remember everything on the sheet, and give it back as near as possible verbatim. I was soon able to do that with fair accuracy. The task was good training. In later years, I was able to read half a page of a book and quote it in public speaking, and sometimes recall it, holus-bolus, years afterwards.

under the bed another container which never froze

In spite of the war, life went on and parish duties had to be done. Indeed, in war time parish duties were often heavier than usual. In Newfoundland villages, for example, official telegrams bringing tidings of another lad dead or missing were often given to the minister to deliver.

Yet the normal pattern of parish routine continued. In 1916 when the war still seemed at a grim stalemate, father finished his pastorate in Bonavista and was moved across Bonavista Bay to Wesleyville.

Wesleyville was a thriving fishing village, the home port of a large fleet of vessels which sailed each year to the Labrador. It was the home also of some of the most famous Newfoundland sea-captains and seal hunters: the Winsors, the Blackwoods, the Keans. As a Methodist circuit, Wesleyville was the main point of a three point charge. A couple of miles south was the small village of Brookfield, and a couple of miles south from Brookfield was another small village, Valleyfield.

Once again we did without a horse. Indeed there were few carriage rigs anywhere in that locality. Roads fit for a carriage seldom extended beyond the village limits. Father did a lot of walking.

In Wesleyville, like a farmer with a big barn and a small house, we had a magnificent church, but a parsonage poorer than any we had previously known. The church was comparatively new, gothic in design, with large windows and a seating capacity of 900. The parsonage was an old building inadequate for our family. The children doubled up in beds; the servant girl had a tiny room to herself. There was a minister's study, a single room added on to the back; but it was terribly cold in winter.

We did have, as in other houses, a standard parsonage fixture, a hall stove. Its pipe went up through the ceiling to the hall upstairs, and did something to spread heat through the house. To help the fire last all night we used hard coal (anthracite); but that was terribly expensive and we resorted to it only on the coldest nights of the year.

In spite of all, we managed, and I have no recollection of discomfort, save the natural discomforts we took for granted. We could, for example, wake up on a winter's morning to find that the water in the wash jug was frozen. (There was another container under the bed which never froze. In those days we had no inside toilet.) But if the water was frozen, so what! We had calf skins or hooked rugs on the floor, and we would soon be down to the kitchen where the good old cook stove shed a warmth that defied even Newfoundland winters.

We had the usual barn, and hayloft, though we kept neither horse nor cow. Few people along that barren shore kept a cow—there was no pasture. Most families which took the trouble to get their own milk kept goats. They could thrive where cows would starve, and unlike cows, they were not susceptible to a prevalent enemy of the time: tuberculosis.

We kept two or sometimes three milk goats; we followed the same pattern of care that we had with our cow. In the morning I would milk them and then let them loose in the woods, fifty feet beyond the back of our house, and in the evening I would fetch them home, milk them and put them in the barn for the night.

In the spring each goat would have a kid, or perhaps two kids, and we would sell them, bring them on for milking, or kill them for food. I not only looked after the goats, but also killed the kids, skinned them and cut them up for eating.

Wesleyville brought us, in acute form, one problem. Nowhere in our life so far had we ever had a tap for water in our house. But in Wesleyville we had not even a useable well; and the nearest pond was over a hill.

Fortunately Newfoundland has a considerable rainfall. To catch soft water for washing we had barrels under the eaves troughs. And as the church with its slate roof was right next to the parsonage, we could get water with no taint of tar. But for drinking and cooking, and sometimes for washing too, in winter or in dry spells, we had to bring it all from the pond over the hill. One person with a hoop could carry two buckets, slopping water as he went; but for us father fixed up a barrow—that is, a flour barrel sawed off at the second hoop and fitted with handles extending at each side. As I was five years older than my next brother, Claude, I had short handles to give me most of the load, and Claude had longer handles to lighten his. Together we could bring back nearly half a barrel at a time. It beat carrying buckets.

When our family moved to Wesleyville in 1916, I was not quite a newcomer to that community. One of father's brothers, our Uncle George, was Wesleyville's chief storekeeper and outfitter of ships. In the summer of 1914, I had gone to Wesleyville for a visit with my cousins. The older boys had already gone, one to Canada, one to the U.S. But the younger two, one just a year older than I, were busy with minor chores in their father's business. It was my first time away from home and I had a touch of homesickness; but nevertheless I had an exciting time.

To begin with, Uncle George had an unused schooner, stripped of her sails and lying at anchor just outside a little cove where his wharf and warehouse stood. My youngest cousin and I would be sent off now and then to board the schooner, pump out the bilge and see if everything was all right. Actually, we went out many more times than were necessary, and we not only inspected the schooner, we would climb the rigging to the masthead and swing around the ropes like young monkeys.

Uncle George also had a fine motor boat for bringing freight from the public wharf. He did not have just a three horsepower one-lunger. He had a two cylinder ten horsepower engine with batteries (four of them wired together) and spark plugs. The engine, it is true, did not have a starter—one got it going by rotating the heavy flywheel. Nor did it have a reverse gear. But that did not bother us. I soon learned a trick, at which my cousins were adept, to slow the engine almost to a stop and then throw the switch at the right time to fire the cylinders in the opposite direction. We could move that boat back and forth as skillfully as now can be done by the gears we take for granted.

So it was in Wesleyville that I learned to climb up and down the rigging of a schooner and to operate and service that new marvel, a motor engine.

Father's pastorate in Wesleyville lasted four years; but I was home only three. By that time I had finished as much schooling as was possible in a Newfoundland outport. Passing the senior grade in the Wesleyville school gave me the right to go on to the Methodist College in St. John's and take the A.A. (Associate of Arts) diploma. That credential qualified one to teach in an outport school, or to enter a Canadian university. My sisters Millicent and Kathleen had preceded me. At that time the Newfoundland government annually gave four scholarships of $100.00 each to the four top graduates of

when the girls first left home, somehow the cash was at hand

the outport schools. In their respective years both Millicent and Kathleen won that scholarship. Millicent had set off for the Methodist College in her fifteenth year. Kathleen, though a year younger than I, had passed me in school and reached the senior grade a year earlier than I. She left before she had reached her fourteenth birthday. Both the girls were very bright students. Compared to them I was a laggard.

One mystery has always escaped me: by what alchemy of discipline and sacrifice were our parents, struggling always with sparse resources, able to come up with the money to start the family off to college? In later years we could help one another somewhat, or get a job to trade time for money. But when the girls first left home somehow the cash was at hand. It was not much, but what was necessary was ready. One thing was clear from the beginning—our parents had not thought that we would stay at the level of outport schools; they expected us to go on to college. Father and mother were a remarkable pair.

As a boy I had an advantage over my sisters; I was able to accumulate some savings of my own. In 1918, my last summer at home, I went fishing in the summer vacation. I was taken on by a neighbour, Bill Saintsbury, a jack of all trades. In the summer he went handlining, that is, fishing with a line having a single hook baited with, say, clams or herring. Sometimes we would turn to jigging. In jigging the line has a lead weight in the shape of a fish and two hooks with no bait. The fisherman lowers this to the bottom of the sea, pulls it up a short distance and then jigs it up and down in hope of snagging some codfish from a passing school.

We used to go several miles out to sea to fish over some promising shoals, the habitat of codfish. We did not have to row; we had an engine. But we would start early in the morning. I used to get up at 5 a.m. and sometimes not get back till late afternoon.

In the course of the summer we had some good fishing and once or twice some very rough water.

I can remember times when the seas were rolling in from storms

45

elsewhere and the waves were huge without breaking. At one moment we would be at the bottom of the trough and it would be just as though we were marooned in a valley of water. We could see nothing but water, water everywhere. Yet at the crest of the next wave our vision would be everywhere to the horizon; inshore, we could see the distant headlands. Fortunately, I was used to knocking about in boats and was not troubled with that dreadful scourge, sea-sickness.

I do not remember how much I made handlining that summer. In any case, I never saw a cent of it. To save me from wasting my substance on the temptations of Wesleyville, Bill Saintsbury gave the money not to me but to father. And father salted it down for the Methodist College.

Two other chances for me to put by a little cash came with jobs at the Wesleyville church.

The first job was pumping the pipe organ. That was a huge instrument, with air pressure provided by long-handled bellows operated by the sole available energy—muscle power. I became the pump motor. For this humble task I was paid twenty cents a Sunday. But twenty cents a Sunday for fifty-two Sundays was over ten dollars; and ten dollars was not to be despised.

One diversion that I permitted myself while I had that job I must mention with due contrition. On one occasion I had to hire another boy to pump for me. I told him that the job was hard work; but he was confident that anything I could do he could do better.

The organ bellows operated by having a valve that opened and closed with the pumping strokes. I tied the valve open. My friend had to pump in a frenzy and even then could scarcely get up enough pressure to keep the organ operating. I thought that it was a great joke. What he thought, it is wiser not to repeat.

My second church job was on a different scale. The Wesleyville church had a lighting system that was, at the time, the last word in efficiency. It used gasoline, but not in individual gasoline lamps. A tank of gasoline in the basement was kept under pressure by a foot pump. The gasoline was piped to a generator in a little room off the vestibule. A small part of the liquid gasoline was bled off to make a flame which would heat the generator and change the liquid into gas. The pressure then carried the gas to individual lamps which burned with an asbestos mantle, like today's Coleman lanterns.

The system of transforming liquid gasoline into gas was effective in producing brilliant light. But, perhaps because the devices were new, they were dangerous. The Wesleyville caretaker—something less than a mechanical genius—had three minor fires; and the congregation was becoming afraid of a disaster.

At the time, I was about fourteen or fifteen years old and intensely interested in anything mechanical. Someone on the official board suggested that I could handle the equipment. So I was employed, not as the regular janitor but as the mechanic for the lighting system. For that I got ten dollars a month, which was also salted down by my father.

I got one fringe benefit. In the basement I found some of the old individual gasoline lamps, discarded for the new system. By cannibalizing parts I was able to make all the lamps we needed in the parsonage, and they served us until we left for the next pastorate.

My final boyhood job came after I had finished my last year at the Wesleyville school and was waiting to set off for the Methodist College, St. John's and the world. For the summer months I went to Greenspond, an island a few miles south of Wesleyville, to take a job as a sort of grease monkey or boy-of-all-work at the A.J. House Woodworking Company. A. J. House was my first cousin Arthur. The story is that just as he was beginning his business on a ragged shoe-string, his lawyer, or someone, made a typing error and incorporated the company with the name spelt "House." And so it has remained for his branch of the family.

Whether that story be fact or fiction, Arthur was a very competent businessman and a very clever mechanic. In Greenspond his company made doors, window sills, moulding and all sorts of finished woodwork. His entire plant was powered by two stationary engines; they were large and heavy with drive wheels perhaps four feet in diameter. They ran on kerosene and were linked by rubber belting to the machinery through the building.

We had a variety of machines. A large circular saw cut logs into boards. Because I was new, I used to stand at the lower end of the carriage which hauled the logs up to the saw. I stood all day in a steady cloud of sawdust. On a couple of occasions when we were pressing the saw too hard with green wood, the saw overheated, buckled and then threw back the log as if it had been fired out of a cannon. If a log had hit me, it would have squashed me like a fly. But that seemed, like storms at sea, to be part of the normal hazard of work that had to be done. No one thought twice about it.

We had other saws for other work, including a thirteen-foot band-saw to run curves. We had lathes, mortice and tenon machines, planers, sanding machines, etc. It was part of my job to look after the two big stationary engines, and to see that they did not waste valuable time by conking out during working hours. But they were simple in design, and Art soon taught me all I needed to know to keep them running.

Art also had, for odd jobs, a small motor boat with a one-lunger engine which had an annoying tendency to stop breathing altogether. I got that engine in good running order, and in a way had a boat of my own.

All that summer I was doing work that I liked—with some exceptions. I had sparse enthusiasm for the times when we were carrying eight foot logs, and I rubbed my shoulders bare. But again, that went with the job.

Art, I think, was surprised at the way I took to machinery. He probably gave me the job as a favour to my father rather than with any great expectancy of my performance. At any rate, while he had promised only to start me at $20 a month, at the end of the month he gave me $40. And so with board at $15 a month I managed during the summer to add another little bit to the family fortunes.

At the end of August I left Greenspond and went back to Wesley-ville to spend a few busy days getting ready for the great trip ahead. I was ready in good time to take the little coastal steamer for St. John's—for me the gateway of the world and the starting point of my joust with destiny.

I was in a measure aware that I had finished an epoch in my life. Yet when I said good-bye to my parents on the public wharf at Wesleyville—my mother bravely wiping away an unruly tear—I had no thought that though they would have over thirty years left to live, never again would I have more than a few fleeting occasions to be even a visitor in their home. I did not know how abruptly I was breaking ties with that secure centre of my life, my home. But as the years went on I knew that most of what was worthwhile in my life had been nurtured there.

I did know that I was at last starting on my own. I was scared and exhilarated: scared that I might somehow make shipwreck of life and bring disgrace on my family; exhilarated because I intended somehow to triumph over every handicap (I felt myself burdened with them) and touch the family heart with pride.

Chapter 4:

On My Own

*exploring St. John's
and the marvels
of city life*

The trip from Wesleyville to St. John's was in reality an ocean voyage. Though the steamer docked in port after port to load and unload cargo and passengers, it had to cross three large bays and to round three stormy capes stretching far out into an ocean unbroken for almost two thousand miles.

In one port where the steamer docked, I went ashore with a friend whom I had just met on the trip. He was a returned soldier, and in my eyes a bit of a hero. We went to visit one of the soldier's army buddies who lived in that village, and the two ex-soldiers kept on talking. I was nervous but would not let myself appear concerned.

When we heard the steamer's warning whistle we were too late. By the time we arrived the steamer had moved out from the wharf. Fortunately the harbour was small with little room for manoeuvering. The steamer had to back slowly and then wheel around to head out to the harbour's mouth. We waved frantically to a small boy in a boat. Rowing furiously, he picked us up and managed to reach the steamer just as it could have put on speed.

The mate was on the bridge. When he saw us waving he slowed the ship till we rowed alongside and climbed up a lowered ladder.

He dressed us down and said that he was fining us five dollars each for delaying the ship. I doubt if he could. At any rate, we heard no more about the matter.

But to me it was a near thing. I could ill afford even five dollars of unnecessary expense. I feared to think of my calamity if I were left stranded in a strange village with only my college money to squander. How I would be messing things up at the beginning of my venture forth to conquer the world!

the deluge
would almost
outdo Niagara

One other memory, vivid and still evocative, is of keeping vigil on deck as the steamer made its careful way into St. John's harbour. We were due to arrive early in the morning on a day that promised to be dull and cold. I was up at 4 A.M. watching as the world got light again. I was the only passenger on deck, but I was so fascinated by the prospect of sailing into that historic harbour, I had to be there to see.

As we steamed toward the shore, it seemed that we were heading toward an unbroken barrier of precipice. Then as we neared we could suddenly see where the opening was, where one headland hid the other giving the appearance of a solid stretch of rocky shore.

I stood in the bow of the steamer enchanted as we passed through the famous Narrows, with the frowning cliffs above, into one of the finest harbours in the world. I saw the steamers and the sailing ships dotting the waters or tied up at the docks. And on the hillsides stretching away from the shore I could see the city, to me an enormous extension of buildings, one of which was to be my new home.

My imagination was kindled as I thought what a mystery life was, not only for me but for all the vast tribe of human beings. I wondered who all these people were, waking up in that great city, what they would be doing today and if I could know them one by one what would their problems and troubles be? Was there anybody else as puzzled as I?

This sort of reflection was, I admit, not new to me. Many times before that morning on the steamer I had been given to puzzled meditation about the strangeness of our existence, the mystery of our own little being in the infinity of our universe.

A few years earlier my father had given me a little book, *Astronomy for Amateurs,* by the French Astronomer, Flammarion. Coming to me at an impressionable age, it was one of the most seminal books I had ever read. It moved me out from the world that had been my home. The spacious firmament on high, the spangled heavens, and the unwearied sun were no longer the centre of creation; they were tiny atoms in an infinite abyss of immeasurable space. And the firm earth on which I stood spun its lonely way in the awful void of a limitless universe.

I was left with a lifetime wonder, and the unanswered question, "What is man?" I was saved from pessimism and atheism by the conviction that the mind which would explore such infinities must have ranges outspanning a merely physical system of atoms and molecules.

More than sixty years have rolled away since I stood in the bow of that steamer peering at the signs of life in the first city I had ever seen, and wondering at the swarming little creatures that crowded there. I am as fascinated and as perplexed now as I was then.

Coming to live in St. John's was for me like moving into a new order of life. From outport village to city, I had moved miles in space but I had also moved years in time.

It is difficult now to realize that I had grown up, not only with no radio and no TV—no one else then had them—but I had never spoken over a telephone, I had never turned on an electric light, I had never lived in a house with running water and I had never ridden in an automobile.

I well recall the first time I did ride in an automobile. Shortly after I arrived in St. John's I went to see a good friend of my father's, Jim Pratt (brother of the poet E. J. Pratt). He was known to all the Howse children as the sender at Christmas of the most marvelous parcels including such exotic items as a turkey or a bundle of grapefruit. The first time grapefruit came, we were unsure what they were and guessed that they might be a kind of overgrown orange.

Pratt invited me to a Saturday lunch and after lunch took me out for a drive a few miles to a little village called Topsail. Coming back at one point where there was a reasonably smooth road the speedometer registered thirty miles an hour. I was thrilled. I had never travelled so fast in all my life. Pratt had a big black Willys-Knight, one of the prestige automobiles of the time. To whiz along the road at such a speed in such a magnificent vehicle thrilled me to no end. That was one of the things I had to tell in my first letter back home.

St. John's provided me with another momentous first. Up to that time, I had never seen a flush toilet, apart from those on a steamer pumped by hand. The College Home—as we called the residential building—had toilets already ancient. The water was in a bowl high up on the wall. The contraption was operated by pulling a long chain, and the deluge that came down would almost outdo Niagara.

The first time I performed the operation I thought that I had burst a water main.

Like the other newcomers to the city, I quickly adapted to the new gadgets, and could soon weave all the new experiences into the common fabric of a daily life. The College Home must have been a large, old family house, converted for college uses. I was on the third floor in a room in which there were three beds; but my roomates were congenial and we managed all right. As I recall we did not fuss even about the food. The fare was simple but adequate, spiced by our voracious appetites. In any case, college authorities would have told us that in the Methodist fashion we were to exemplify plain living and high thinking.

The discipline was fairly rigorous. We had prayers on various occasions which we endured with mild stoicism. We were paraded to church on Sunday morning but were free to make our own choice in the evening.

One of my most satisfactory achievements was that I made the rugby team. I was a bit of a runt. I was five feet eight and skinny as a rake, weighing 139 pounds. I made it for one reason—I was fast. I was thrilled to be on the team and yet terrified that somehow I might break a bone and lose my year—a possibility that seemed to me an irretrievable calamity. The worst that happened to me was that once when I unfortunately got underneath in a scrim. I burst a blood vessel on my lungs. The doctor soon reassured me that I need not worry.

How much the year cost, and with what resources my father paid the bills I do not know. Millicent and Kathleen had preceded me. The scholarships my sisters had won, plus the money I had managed to earn, must have been considerably less than the cost for three students at a boarding school—even with the low rates for minister's children. I do not know what share of that burden my father had to scrape together so that I could go on with my education instead of stepping out of school to some job—perhaps fishing—in Wesleyville. But at least I have this measure of satisfaction: I was then sixteen years of age, and that was the last time I ever took a penny from home. Perhaps I was the better off in that, though my father could not send me to university, he could give me the will to go.

In those days we got along on an incredibly small amount of cash. I kept account of my expenses. In a little booklet which I still have somewhere, I noted such expenditures as an evening paper, one cent;

collars cleaned (in those days they had to be starched) two cents each; theatre, five cents. I had one entry on a more lavish scale. A group of entertainers came to St. John's, some sort of vaudeville with a chorus line. I had heard of such wickedness in far away places. Now I thought that I should see for myself. I spent seventy-five cents for admission. But I rarely let myself go with such abandon for things that were not essential to the nobler ambitions.

Make no mistake, I was not mummified by any monkish ways. I just didn't have the cash. A song popular at the time ran this way, "When I was twenty one ... I didn't have lots of money; but I did have lots of fun." That described many of us. Everyone was poor as all the rest. And we were perhaps as happy as any generation in my lifetime.

As to my education, which I must not forget was the real reason for my going to St. John's, we were fortunate that the Methodist College had high standards. The Principal was an old-fashioned English headmaster who would tolerate nothing less than excellence, and the teachers were competent and dedicated. Some of the pupils came from village schools which left much to be desired, others from schools such as that at Blackhead which did first rate work, because of first rate school masters. Those who came from such schools and finished at the Methodist College were as well taught as those from any school anywhere in Canada. When they went to Canadian universities they had no difficulty in holding their own with their fellow students.

I finished my single year at the college and got my A.A. diploma. I even got a minor prize, a cheque for twenty-five dollars. At the graduation ceremony it came as a surprise because I had not been informed beforehand. I and some friends were occupying ourselves at the rear with a great lack of attention when Sir Richard Squires, chairman of the ceremonies, read out my name. I did not even hear it until one of my comrades whispered loudly, "Ernie, that's you."

I got up in some confusion and made my astonished way to the platform. It was not my fate however, to hold on to that money for

*I had heard
of such wickedness
in far away places*

long. The next day the principal of the College Home had me sign over the cheque to credit my account at the college.

Perhaps it was just as well. If I had had all that money to spend on myself, who knows to what evil ways I might have been inveigled? Better men than I have been corrupted by riches.

With the A.A. from the Methodist College I could now be admitted to a Canadian university. I intended to study law. Indeed I had—modestly—decided to come back to Newfoundland, enter politics and take over the job as Premier. In flight of wilder fantasy I remembered that a flamboyant Newfoundland politician had said that the Premier of Newfoundland who took Newfoundland into Confederation could become Prime Minister of Canada.

But while I now had the academic qualifications to enter university, I did not have the financial resources. I had to trade time for money. I would have to find an interim job in which I could save enough to get started.

The Principal of the college told me that he had been asked by a bank to recommend a boy to come on its staff, and that he was willing to recommend me. I was surprised but I did not want to spend my life in a bank. So I turned down the offer. I was hoping to get something with high wages, and I was quite willing for it to be hard labour, if necessary.

Also I kept in mind that enduring resource of our family—school teaching. If I could get a reasonably good school, I might make a thousand dollars a year, maybe more. I decided to look around a bit. So I went back to Wesleyville, by the same steamer on which I had travelled it seemed so long before.

It chanced that this was the year in which my father finished his Wesleyville pastorate. He was going back to the Burin peninsula, to the largest town in that part of the island, Grand Bank.

So I helped pack our belongings, a task in which father and mother were expert since they had been doing it every three or four years for their whole working lifetime, and I went with the family to their new home.

The manse in Grand Bank was quite a change from that at Wesleyville. It was new, having been built a year or so earlier, it was large and well appointed and, wonder of wonders, it had running water. The town still had no water system; the parsonage had a zinc-lined water tank up in the attic, and a large single-handled pump in the basement. From our own well we would pump the water to the tank

54

and from there gravity would take over. It was a big improvement on buckets and hand-barrow. But even so one did not waste water. Incidentally, the sewage outlet was just a pipe running to the sea.

Grand Bank was a centre of wealth. It made its money not only by fishing off the Grand Banks but also by freighting fish and other cargo to Spain and the Caribbean in huge three-masted or even four-masted sailing vessels. One Grand Bank family had, I think, sixteen of these monarchs of the seas, an impressive fortune in itself.

better men than I have been corrupted by riches

For the summer months, I stayed in Grand Bank. I got a number of odd jobs, once as a carpenter reparing a warehouse, and at different times by working as a longshoreman bringing freight from coastal steamers anchored off-shore.

Grand Bank had a poor harbour. Steamers which brought mail and freight could not venture into the public wharf, except in calm seas. They anchored outside. We went out in boats to bring in whatever cargo there was for whatever merchant we served. With the steamers pitching and the boat below pitching even more, and with barrels and crates being lowered over the side and somehow landing in the boats without staving them in, unloading freight was sometimes quite a job. However, for this we got high pay, I think seventy-five cents an hour. If I could keep up that rate, it wouldn't take me long to get to university.

Another job for which I got fairly high pay was loading one of those three-masted schooners with fish. The vessel was tied up to a pier and the fish—split, salted, and dried—were dumped down into the hold in wagon loads. They were not in any containers. When the load was dumped we would rush to the pile, pick up armfuls (yaffels), and stack them in layers, to fill the cavernous hold of the immense vessel. The days were hot, the air down in the hold was stifling, and the work was hard. The fact that the air was filled with salt didn't make things any better. It was the worst of all filling up the last six feet. As the level rose, we could not stand upright under the deck, but had to crouch and throw in the fish until they closed the gap. This was called "lungering up." We earned our wages.

The summer jobs served for the moment, but I was looking for something permanent. One idea that tempted me was the possibility of signing on as an able-bodied seaman, and spending a year or two on one of those magnificent four-masted schooners. The pay was reasonably good, and made better by the fact that at sea there was little chance for spending money. I was old enough to go, young enough to be excited by the adventure.

I did not get far with my notion. Both father and mother were strongly opposed. They feared, first, that life on a sailing ship would be too tough for me; and second, that if I did settle into a seafarer's life, I might lose all ambition to go to university.

I was not bent on being a sailor; I was just fascinated by those marvellous ships. So I dropped my brief idea.

The ship on which I was told I might get a berth, not long after was caught in a storm and foundered at sea.

I have lived with certain lingering regret that I did not take that chance of life on one of those fascinating queens of the ocean. Had I done so—and survived—I would today be among a very small company of my present day peers who have served as a sailor before the mast.

Chapter 5:

Outport Teacher

*isolation and challenge
on Newfoundland's
northeast coast*

Having ruled out life at sea, and with no other prospect in sight, I turned my thoughts again to school teaching. Through father, I enquired of the Methodist Superintendent of Schools about the possibility of a school on the Labrador, somewhere in touch with a Grenfell mission. The reply came that Labrador had no opening, but that a place called La Scie on the northeast coast of Newfoundland wanted a master for its upper room.

I had never heard of La Scie, and small wonder. It was a settlement of perhaps a couple of hundred inhabitants, ambitiously called souls, on an isolated stretch of rough shoreline between Notre Dame Bay and White Bay, at the base of Newfoundland's long northern peninsula. By coincidence, it was only eight miles north of the place where my father had begun his first pastorate, the erstwhile mining town of Tilt Cove. As nothing more romantic was within my horizon, I offered to take that vacant post.

I was seventeen.

The local school board paid a salary of $500. Because I had an A.A. certificate central funds would pay "augmentation" as it was called, of $500. This total of $1000 for ten months seemed not too bad. I was confident that I could save a substantial sum.

Getting from one place in Newfoundland to another always involved a circuitous voyage: this time two voyages by steamer with an interlude of travel by train. I went from Grand Bank, around Cape Race and the "Graveyard of the Atlantic" to St. John's, then took trains to the end of a spur line at Lewisporte at the bottom of Notre Dame Bay, and there caught a steamer meandering her weekly route to the Labrador.

The steamer did not call at La Scie, which had neither harbour nor public wharf adequate for anything but a small schooner. She discharged her La Scie cargo at the nearest navigable port, Tilt Cove. Even Tilt Cove did not then have a suitable dock. The steamer just dropped anchor at a safe distance from land, lowered a lifeboat and dumped into it my trunk and me, some mail and an assortment of parcels for local businesses, and put us ashore.

On land I met the La Scie mailman, waiting with a horse and cart. I transferred to this new locomotion. Laden with a motley assortment of freight we started up a steep hill and jiggled our eight mile journey across a neck of land to the end of the trail—La Scie itself.

La Scie introduced me to a way of life in some respects different from anything in my past. We were not really in the north, but we were far enough north to be cut off from the south by the curtain of winter. When the coastal steamer passed us by heading south on her last trip of the fall season, that was the last traffic for all that northern section of Newfoundland until the first steamer the next spring.

In consequence everything the people needed—all the flour, tea, sugar, all the stocks for the little stores, all the medicines, all the incidentals of community existence—had to be stocked in the fall. Every winter, every family would find itself short of something, and there was only one remedy—do without. Possibly a neighbour could help. In such a community, the spirit of neighbourliness was a lustre that brightened every darkness.

La Scie had to cope with further effects of isolation. Sickness and accidents came, and other troubles such as tooth-aches, of the prolonged agonies of which civilized communities now have no idea.

In La Scie or anywhere near it in those stark days, we had no hospital, no doctor, no trained nurse, no dentist, and certainly no airplane with heroic bush pilots dropping from the skies on errands of mercy. Rescues now possible in the most isolated settlement in the high Arctic were beyond our reach in La Scie.

I remember someone in Grand Bank asking me, "But what if you get appendicitis?" The answer was simple. To get appendicitis was to have "inflammation of the bowels" was to die. No wonder that life expectancy was so much lower then than it is now.

Mail did continue year round. In winter it was picked up from ports farther south, and carried in stages by dog-team. The La Scie mailman would get his mail from Tilt Cove. Trading his pony for his dogs he would travel the same path, kept broken mainly by himself. A couple of times through the winter I made the trip with the mailman. I remember one occasion when we came back from Tilt Cove on a bright moonlit night. The path was good and the dogs could tear at racing speed on the down grades. We would shout and hear the echoes from the hills. Once when we ran under a telegraph wire, the mailman hit it with the whip handle, and the sound, it seemed, travelled for miles, echoing and re-echoing down the wire on the still, cold winter night. The dogs went like mad, and we were wilder than they.

The telegraph wire was our one steady link with the outside world. Even a small community such as La Scie had its telegraph office and an operator expert in Morse code. We could always send a telegram to our families outside, or they could send one to us.

Of course, sending a telegram was reserved for special occasions, such as birth or death. To be told that a telegram had come was to feel an instinctive fear.

The master for the upper room in the La Scie school was a person of some consequence in the community. When I arrived a young man named Max Parsons was the probationer for the Methodist church, and so was my chief. Parsons was slightly older than I, an extremely bright fellow and an extraordinarily good public speaker. He had arrived a little earlier than I and had already taken the village by storm. For a short while we were great friends. Unfortunately Max developed tuberculosis. He managed to catch the last steamer going south for the winter. La Scie then had no minister. Though I did not know it, this was to have consequence for me.

In La Scie I stayed with a family named Bartlett. Abe Bartlett was the manager of a branch store. In earlier years he had been a blacksmith and he still looked it. He was strong as a small elephant, and a most congenial host. He told me that when he had built his first house, at his marriage, he saved something by making in his own forge—one by one—all the nails.

The Bartletts had one son, Ross, almost as husky as his father.

shooting from a small boat in a rough sea requires skill

They also had a daughter who had recently married a village lad. Her mother disapproved of him. I suspected she had aspired to donate her daughter to one of the ministers or school teachers appointed to La Scie, and was miffed that the girl had married only a fisherman.

Mrs. Bartlett was a friendly soul and a good cook and kind to me; but she was one of the greatest gossips I have had the fortune to meet. Ross once said to her, "If you talk like that about other women, they will talk about you."

Mrs. Bartlett, with an air of infinite superiority, replied, "How can they talk about me? I only talk about them because they have done what ought to be talked about."

I found my school work demanding but interesting. During the winter months I had several village boys sent to school in the slack period to brush up on their three Rs. Some of them were as old as I, and one or two were certainly bigger. I suspect that there was some egging-on to see what would happen if any of the big boys took on the teacher. I was a bit worried about that myself. I carried on however, hoping to create the impression that though I might be knocked down, I wouldn't back down.

I also earned good will, I think, by visiting my pupils' homes and getting to know the families. In La Scie, this was new.

I did everything I could think of to be the best teacher the school had ever known. We got through the winter without any trouble, and some at least of the potential troublemakers became my loyal fans.

Outside the school I had a glorious time.

During the winter, I used on Saturdays to go into the woods to cut firewood. I had used an axe since I was old enough to lift one; but I got extra practice that year. We not only had to cut the trees (we did not use saws for felling) we had to load them on the sled we had towed in and pull them back home. As the terrain was hilly we were most of the time either straining to pull the sled uphill, or keeping it from disaster going downhill. For a brake we would put a chain around one of the logs and drag it behind. After we got the logs

60

home we had to saw them, split them and stack them in long rows. It was amazing how much that stove in the kitchen would consume, all the year round.

I used to go out in a rowboat, sometimes by myself, sometimes with friends, to shoot ducks and other sea birds for our larder. I was a reasonably good shot, though not up to many of the men from the village. Shooting from a small boat in a rough sea requires considerably more skill than firing from firm ground.

Coming on Spring, I went one weekend with several friends to a point on the coast several miles east to shoot ducks. We stayed in a "tilt" (shack) built for such expeditions. Across one end of the single room was a built-in bench about six feet wide. The men would sleep at right angles to the wall and thus half a dozen men could sleep on the only bed there was. As the bench was made of small logs flattened only on the top side and as there was no bedding but a blanket or quilt, newcomers would not find it too comfortable.

Further, the heat came from a wood cook-stove which quickly changed from redhot to cold, and which someone had to refill about every hour through the night. My only report is that echo from the French Revolution, "I survived." To make everything all right, the next day we got a hefty batch of ducks, a promise of appetising dinners ahead.

At that time, the northern part of Newfoundland swarmed with prodigious flocks of sea fowl. I have seen ducks like a low, dark cloud, shrouding the seaward skies from horizon to horizon. During my La Scie winter, a Tilt Cove man killed eighty-two ducks with one shot. To know how that was possible you have to know two things: the kind of gun and the method of its use.

The gun would be an enormous old sealing musket made in England a century earlier. The bore would be well over an inch and designed to carry a heavy load of powder and a generous handful of quarter shot. For duck shooting this would be translated into less powder and a larger slug of smaller shot.

When the gun was ready, everything depended on the circumstance. The whole northern sea would be covered with endless square miles of drifting ice, crowding into the shore. Along the edge the receding tide would loosen the pack and leave a winding margin of water, clear and blue, an inviting storehouse of food for passing flights of waterfowl.

Ducks would see those patches of water and swoop down from the

61

heavens till they were packed like a living tapestry. The hunter would hide behind the "ballycater"—high ridges of ice made when the spray dashed over the rocks at the water's edge. At the critical moment he would make some sharp noise, and the ducks as by one reflex would crane their heads. According to his skill (or luck) he would spray small shot over a patch of water crammed with ducks. To kill eighty-two was a remarkable feat but not a record. On one occasion, local tradition affirms, the count went over 100.

The duck hunters would have a small boat, a "rodney" we called it, with a curved keel, preferably banded with whalebone. The rodney could be run over ice like a sled. The instant the gun was fired a couple of men, one on each side, would grab the boat and run into the water to pick up any birds that were merely wounded, before they could recover enough to fly.

Duck hunting on this pattern was not sport but a business of providing the family with food.

My year at La Scie brought a couple of occasions when only good luck, a reasonable amount of savvy and some tough slugging saved me from ending my youthful days in a watery grave.

The first occasion was when with a friend of mine, Leander Gillard, who happened to be teaching at Tilt Cove, I decided to row out to a famous landmark of that northern coastline: Gull Island.

Gull Island is a huge hunk of rock, two thirds of a mile long and less than that in width, half a mile or so off shore at Cape St. John at the north west corner of Notre Dame Bay. It is about 19 miles east from La Scie—miles that are unbroken cliffs, up to five hundred feet high, dropping precipitously to the sea. The whole stretch of shore has not a single break where a boat could find refuge in a storm.

The island has gruesome fame as the scene of one of the most horrible shipwrecks in Newfoundland history. (Some years ago, I wrote that story. A condensed version appeared in 1969 in *Macleans Magazine*).

In brief, the square-rigged sailing vessle, "Queen of Swansea," heading in December 1857 with cargo and passengers from St. John's to Tilt Cove, was driven by storm off her course and while battling her way back in a raging snow storm ran headlong into Gull Island's mountainous cliffs. By chance the schooner grounded on a sloping ledge. The crew got the passengers ashore before the stranded vessel, the coffin for those still aboard, slipped back into the sea and sank.

62

in desperate weather on a barren rock without food

Those who were saved were the unfortunate. In desperate weather on a barren rock, without food and with only snow for water, some of them lasted as long as two weeks. They survived that long only by eating the bodies of those who died first. Some of them, including the indomitable Captain, kept records or wrote farewell notes from which the tragic story was slowly deduced late the next spring, when what was left of their bodies were dug from the ice in which the salt spray had interred them.

Gillard and I wanted to see the scene of the grisly disaster. We knew the lighthouse keeper, Ephraim Whelan from La Scie. Whelan and his wife, with a young man as assistant, got few callers to break the monotony of their rocky perch in the lighthouse. We would be warmly welcomed by the lonely trio.

We borrowed a small rowboat equipped with two pairs of oars (in Newfoundland when one man rowed two oars we called them paddles). We were not daunted by a twenty-mile trip under our own power.

When we arrived, we went to the same sloping ledge where the "Queen" had crashed to her doom. It was the only place on the island where a boat could be safely beached. A winch installed there pulled us up beyond the water line.

The Whelans were glad to see us, and after a meal together Ephraim decided that he could put us to good use. He suggested that since they were short on some supplies after the winter, he would send his wife and his assistant in the lighthouse motorboat to Tilt Cove to buy what they could. Meanwhile we would stay on as his back-up.

It would have been a pleasant interlude, but for a change in the weather. In the afternoon, the light wind of the morning turned into a gale. By the time that Mrs. Whelan should be returning, she knew that no boat could land on Gull Island.

It didn't matter. She had friends to stay with. Gillard and I had intended to stay overnight anyway. So, while we could not communicate, each party knew what the other was doing. Through the night Gillard and I took watches and all was well.

But the storm did not die down overnight. Rather, it increased, with driving gusts of rain reducing visibility so low that we had to start the fog horn.

The storm lasted not only Sunday but went into Monday. It was not till Tuesday morning that the lighthouse boat was able to return from Tilt Cove, and we set out on our long row home.

Our troubles, however, were not over. The lull was only temporary. Before long the wind picked up again, shifting direction so that we had to row into its teeth. We fought a stormy battle every mile back to La Scie, drenched with cold spray, at times with one rowing and the other bailing. Fortunately, we were both under eighteen years of age, in good condition and competent in handling small boats in stormy water. So we made it safely.

all we could do was drift along to the open sea

We reached La Scie with the coming of dark. The folk were glad to see us. From the time we had left on Saturday morning they had no knowledge of where we were, how we were faring, or if we had been drowned at sea. That was the norm in the days before radio.

We learned that no fishing boat had ventured out of the harbour that Tuesday. Some of the fishermen said that if we had not made it they would not have believed that a boat so small as ours could have come through the storm.

For ourselves, we had had a glorious time, and were thrilled with it all. It was then that I began to collect what records I could find about the wreck of the "Queen."

The second occasion when I might have ended my days in the North Atlantic was in the seal hunting season. For centuries, just as people caught fish for food, shot sea birds for food, and killed caribou for food, so in seal-hunting time they would kill seals for food. They counted nothing more unusual about that than in killing the sheep they bred themselves, and nothing more wrong in eating a seal flipper than in eating a lamb chop.

In some seasons the drift of the ice brought large numbers of seals

64

in near shore. Then fishermen in villages near which the seals were passing could go after seals either by walking out over the ice or in boats where there were patches of water.

The families that got seals were fortunate. They would not only have seal meat; they would have the blubber to sell and the hide for making skin boots and snowshoes. To get a few seals in the spring was a welcome addition to the family reserves.

That year the seal-bearing ice was a long distance off and our prospects were not bright. But Gillard and I thought that it would be a good idea for us to go out one Saturday and get a seal or two for the families with whom we lived.

I went over to Tilt Cove on Friday night and stayed with Gillard. He had borrowed a boat much like the one we had before. We set out in the morning with only scattered ice to seaward. What we did not know was that though we were in loose patches of ice, further south a large area in the bay was packed with an ice jam.

Unfortunately, after hours in loose ice, with no seal near except an old one in the water which we missed, a fresh wind blew up. All the ice to the south of us began moving out to sea. Soon we were so caught in the flow that all we could do was to haul our boat up on an ice pan and drift along with the icefield, out of Notre Dame Bay to the open ocean. We sat down in the shelter of our boat, ate a little food sparingly because we were not sure what was our prospect, and began to wonder what would happen to us if the wind kept up.

What would have happened is that we would have gone out to sea with the wind—and the ice—and with little likelihood of ever making it back.

But by good luck, just about dusk the wind slackened and the icepack began to loosen. We were not too far from shore. We pushed the boat into the water wherever we could find channels and where we could not we pulled the boat like a sled over the ice to the next patch. After some strenuous exertion and what seemed a long time we reached a spot of almost clear water stretching to the land. We rowed with gusto toward a little harbour where we could see the lights of a few houses.

It was a place called Snook's Arm. Once upon a time it had been the centre of a whaling industry. But the whaling station had been closed for many years and only a handful of fishing folk remained.

They were as kind to us as people who live off the sea always are to people in distress from the sea. A family which happened to have a spare room, took us in, and after a good meal and a friendly chat we got a good night's rest.

The next morning, Sunday, the ice was back. There was no possibility of rowing back to Tilt Cove. The only thing we could do was to leave our boat and head back through the woods. The distance to Tilt Cove was not great—probably less than ten miles. But this was territory without roads. It was rough, hilly terrain in the early spring when the rivers were beginning to break up and the ponds were unsafe. There would be times when every footstep would be a struggle or a hazard.

We started after breakfast, without a compass, depending only on our sense of direction and on not going too long out of sight of the sea. Sometimes, winding through scrubby trees, we waded through deep snow. Sometimes we were on bare rocky hills. Every now and then we had to find some way to cross a river or a pond. It was a long arduous struggle and at the end of the day we were not yet at the end of the trail. Fortunately we had a full moon, and we had light not only for the day but for most of the night. We reached Tilt Cove past midnight. There I had a "Mug-up" with Gillard and I set off by myself for the remaining eight miles. But that was easy; there was a road, or at least a mailman's trail. I arrived home about three o'clock in the morning. It had been quite a day.

The Bartletts, like Gillard's hosts in Tilt Cove, had gone to bed with no idea where we were. They were apprehensive that we might be in trouble somewhere out on the ice. But they could do nothing except wait and hope. La Scie, and Tilt Cove also, had a telegraph office. If we had not arrived by Monday morning someone would probably have sent a telegram to our parents. But happily by school-time Monday we were at our desks again. A few of our pupils might have borne their sorrow, had we not returned until just a day or so later.

Chapter 6

Testing the Ministry

*learning
the fine art
of the pulpit*

I went to La Scie with one purpose; to save money so that I could go to university and become a lawyer. But the destiny that shapes our ends shaped mine to a pattern that I had not anticipated.

The change began in La Scie. In the Methodist church at that time the only way to become a member was to be "converted." For Methodists that was as essential as for Anglicans to be confirmed. I was not converted and had no sympathy for those who would divide Christians into the saved and the unsaved. But having grown up in a Methodist parsonage, I was to a degree greater than I knew tinctured with a Christian influence. I wanted somehow to identify myself as a Christian, and to be a member of the church, not an outsider.

I decided that as the church had set conversion as the method of admission, I should enter by that door. One Sunday evening when my friend Leander Gillard, who had previously been accepted as a probationer of the Methodist church, was taking the service in the La Scie church, I waited till the appropriate time in the prayer meeting that followed. Then with no appeals for conversion or revival emotion, I quietly got out of my seat, went up to the communion rail and knelt down. In the language of the day, I had "made a decision for Christ."

Gillard, as he told me later, was astonished beyond measure; and so, I am sure, were all the others in that little meeting. But I had a deep satisfaction. Entirely of my own choosing, I had—in the modern phrase—done my own thing. I had made my declaration that to my best understanding and ability I intended to "follow Christ."

My action, which provided the whole village with gossip for the next two weeks, had unexpected consequences. La Scie, since the departure of Max Parsons, had no regular minister. I was soon pressured into filling in for the local preachers who had been carrying on without a probationer. For my first attempt, I read a sermon clipped from an old issue of the "Family Herald and Weekly Star," then a publication scarcely second to Eaton's catalogue in the outhouses of the remoter districts of Newfoundland. The brevity of the newspaper sermon and the speed with which I, in my nervousness, read the thing, meant that the La Scie congregation had the shortest Sunday morning service in living memory.

That was only the beginning. From here and there I began to get more adequate material. I was surprised how many books some of these local preachers had. Further, even in the Newfoundland winter, I got from my father, within a few weeks, a most helpful selection of sermons and sermonic aids. Soon I was not just reading sermons, I was writing them. For my last couple of months, I was both the high school teacher, and in effect the minister.

My father was not only the minister of his Grand Bank congregation. In the wider work of the Methodist church he was also Chairman of the District, as the Methodists called it, in which his parish lay. This meant that, among other duties, he had the responsibility of recruiting probationers for the small congregations which could not independently support their own clergy. And his district had

The Methodist church at La Scie,
where I preached—or rather read—my first sermon.

some demanding mission fields.

From Grand Bank, the southern coast of Newfoundland stretched two hundred miles to Cape Bay, its western extremity. That bleak and sparsely populated shoreline was dotted with a fringe of scattered settlements, each isolated from the other. The whole territory had neither road nor railway to link them to the rest of Newfoundland. Each little harbour had access to the world only by sea.

Near the western end of this bleak strip of coastline, the largest settlement among settlements all small, was the old and sturdy community of Burgeo. For generations through good times and bad, Burgeo had maintained its independant and obscure existence and would likely be still unknown but for one adventitious event. Once upon a time—a time somewhat later than mine—a bewildered whale managed to imprison itself in a Burgeo inlet just about big enough to be a whale's bathtub. The brutality of certain villagers in making a target of the creature, and the fury Farley Mowat poured out in his book, *A Whale for the Killing,* made Burgeo for a few days the cynosure of international news.

In the spring of 1921, Farley and the whale were as yet undreamed of. Burgeo had an honoured place as the centre of a loyal little Methodist community looking to its leaders to find them a minister. The former probationer—a young man whose dedication had more than compensated for his inexperience—was leaving to begin university studies in Canada. My father had to find a successor. And in that he had a problem.

The Burgeo Methodist mission field was not limited to Burgeo itself. It included two other outlying settlements: Ramea, a tiny island, or more strictly a cluster of islands, about 15-20 miles to the southeast; and Otter's Point, another island, about 25 miles to the west. Thus the parish in total covered three communities, spread over almost fifty miles of mostly vacant coastline where the inshore waters were sprinkled with visible rocks and invisible "sunkers" that remained a constant peril even to the experienced navigator. Only a few years after my time, the Methodist Superintendent of Missions was drowned while on a visit to Burgeo.

The Burgeo minister would have few qualifications more desirable than the ability to travel when necessary on his own to his appointed duties. It may well be that my familiarity with boats was counted as an extra, enhancing the meagreness of my ministerial qualifications.

Whatever the reason, my father told me that he had no

probationer to fill that Burgeo post, and asked me whether, after my La Scie apprenticeship, I would be willing to go to Burgeo as a probationer on trial for a year.

I do not know what led me to say yes. It may have been in part that I was not aware what would be demanded of me. It may be that I was buoyed up by my father's confidence in me. And certainly one element enticing me was the prospect of carrying on something like a marine mission. Perhaps too, a final element was an inclination which was to remain with me all through my life: never to refuse a task just because I was afraid of it.

So I did accept my father's proposal. I did not look upon it as a commitment to the ministry. I knew other young men who had served as supply ministers, in Newfoundland or out West, and who went on to other callings. I was willing to see whether or not the ministry was for me.

Prior to the Burgeo proposal, I had taken for granted that I would be staying on at La Scie for another year. The villagers, I think would have been pleased. They made it heartwarmingly clear that they were glad I had come and sorry I was to leave. I went to La Scie with some apprehension as to how well I would fit in; I left with a good feeling that I would be remembered as a friend. I had immensely enjoyed my year and felt a real sadness when the day came to say goodbye and wind up what would prove to be my only attempt at school teaching.

From La Scie I went back to Grand Bank. I spent a few weeks with my family, and filled in time so far as I could doing such odd jobs as I could get. Father arranged that I assist him at some of his services. My inaugural appearance was not on a Sunday but on a Wednesday night preaching service—an extra hour of worship sustained only by the inexhaustible piety of the older Methodists. When we got back home my father told me, with great satisfaction, of the comment of one of the Grand Bank oligarchy, an octogenarian who was one of his closest personal friends and an alabaster pillar of the church. The old man said that he was "agreeably surprised." My father was pleased. I was a bit skeptical; I thought that this praise might have measured not the excellence of my performance but the poverty of his expectations.

On the first of August, 1921, I again took a coastal steamer and headed west to begin my work in Burgeo. I faced a formidable task with the audacity of ignorance. I had to preach twice each Sunday, morning and evening. In the afternoon, I had to teach an adult Bible Class—to people who had been studying the Bible all their lifetime. After the Sunday service I had to conduct a prayer meeting, at which only the faithful remained but which the faithful would not let die.

On Wednesday evening I had to conduct the week night preaching service; and this required a full length sermon just at the Sunday services did.

I was eighteen years of age. Until a few weeks earlier I had never in my life preached a sermon nor made a public address—with the notable exception of my six year old performances in Blackhead. How I plunged in and maintained the routine of three sermons a week I find it hard now to understand. The New Testament and the more colourful stories of the Old Testament were my richest resource. I am even more bewildered to recall that I wrote my sermons by hand. I turned up one of them recently while cleaning out some files, and judged it a passable sermon; at least, thanks to the Newfoundland schools and my home, my syntax was in order. I managed only by working long hours, and making good use of the evenings and the nights, for there were not many evening events in Burgeo.

I managed also in my first year at Burgeo to write a fairly long story, a tale of disaster at sea, which I sold—for eight dollars—to a paper called *Onward,* and which is still at the United Church Archives in Toronto.

A young people's picnic in Burgeo.
In the boat we had tholes (toe pins) rather than oarlocks.
Life preservers were, as always, non-existent.

Despite appearances, this old tub at Burgeo is tight—
the seams are well caulked with tar.
The stern has a cutout in it for a sculling oar.

In addition to the preaching, I was supposed to visit my Burgeo parishioners at least once a month; if I didn't, some people would grumble that I was neglecting my duties. Outside my pastoral duties I was called upon for a bewildering variety of personal services. I had a special licence to conduct marriages; and I had to conduct funerals which in those days meant a service in church—with yet another sermon. I sometimes wrote letters for the illiterate. I helped them transact their business. On one occasion I remember drafting (I suspect imperfectly) a will for a man who was dying. I even helped draft a petition to be sent to the House of Parliament asking for repairs to the public wharf.

Most exciting of all, I occasionally acted as assistant when the Burgeo general practitioner had to perform an operation.

The doctor, a young man named Cecil Kean (whose father was one of Newfoundland's most celebrated sea captains) had served his first years in medical practice on the battlefields of France. Consequently he was a first class surgeon, and later had a large practice in St. John's. He was probably the only man anywhere along that coastline with a university degree.

I have vivid memories of times when I was called in to his aid. The first was when he had to cut off the middle finger of a lady to save

72

her from gangrene. The operating table was a union of the kitchen and dining room tables in the house where I boarded. My landlady (in her seventies) was the general assistant providing linen, the boiled water for sterilizing and whatever else was needed. A neighbouring lady administered the anaesthetic—chloroform dripped onto a pad over the patient's mouth. I just handed Dr. Kean whatever he wanted and did whatever he told me.

Unfortunately the lady who was administering the chloroform became so interested in what we were doing that she tipped the bottle too much and ran the drip to a stream.

Suddenly the patient went stiff as a board. I thought we had killed her. But Dr. Kean was unflappable. Working swiftly but coolly he gave her a shot of adrenalin, and pumped her arms up and down, and in no time extracted from her a deep groan. With that sign of life we went on with the operation. Such was my introduction to the art of surgery.

Another time I helped Doctor Kean cut off most of the flesh of the forearm of a man who had accidentally shot himself while alone in the woods. He had to walk back home by himself, and after waiting for days in a fruitless attempt to have his wife adequately dress the wound, had to be hauled something like thirty miles on a sled to Burgeo. By that time gangrene had set in. To push a finger in the flesh was like poking it in dough; the impression would stay. Dr. Kean, however, tried first to save the arm by cutting off only as much flesh as was absolutely beyond recovery. Later he had to amputate the arm at the elbow.

On that operation I was almost myself a casualty. The blood did not bother me, but the smell did. On two or three occasions I barely managed to remain on my feet without throwing up all I had eaten the week before. Somehow I survived; and as the operation happened on a Sunday I sandwiched it—barely—between the end of my morning service and the beginning of my Bible class.

This was an aspect of ministerial training not on the curriculum of any theological seminary. It was clear in the minds of the villagers and myself that a minister was at everybody's service, whatever the need.

The other times of excitement in my Burgeo years were my trips to Ramea and Otter's Point. Ramea probably did not have two dozen Methodists; but they had been there a long time and the Burgeo minister was supposed to visit them once every three months. Otter's

Point, of which the small population was almost entirely Methodist, was slated for a Sunday's service once every month. The ministerial visit there usually lasted not just the weekend but the best part of the week.

My trips to Ramea were usually brief. On my second visit in late November, 1921, however, I was stormbound there for a week. I had to preach not only twice on Sunday but every night from Monday till Friday. I had no notes for such a series (at that time I did not take notes to the pulpit; I drafted the full text in my study). Despite my deficiencies almost every Ramea Methodist turned up for every service. My admiration for Methodist stamina was unbounded.

Normally I went to Ramea and came back with the mailman who used to make two trips a week to the families along a section of that shore. He had a skiff, that is to say a small schooner, with a jib, foresail and mainsail. As the coarse canvas sails of that time were heavy, handling them was quite a job for one man, particularly if he was at the same time steering the boat. I was always a willing, and welcome, crewman.

In Ramea, the lady I stayed with—a widow with one son; her husband had drowned at sea—had in her garden a tiny potato patch

The "skiff" which carried all the mail along the Burgeo coast.
The minister travelled as crewman to Ramea and Otter's Point.

*The house at Ramea at which the minister stayed.
The rock I helped to blow up, and the outhouse,
are both hidden from view.*

made tinier by a huge rock perhaps three feet square. It was a nuisance; and in a brash moment I suggested to her that I could blow up that thing with gunpowder.

I got a young man from the village, and we borrowed a star drill and a maul and pounded a hole deep in the centre of that rock. Then we filled the hole half full of gunpowder—a commodity available anywhere in Newfoundland outports—and packed the top with powdered brick.

Then we covered everything with some old sails and firewood logs, rolled out a long fuse and lit it with a match.

Our intentions were good. But neither I nor my friend, though we had both seen such an operation, knew too much about what we were doing. So it was more by luck than by skill that we did so much good with so little damage. We shattered the rock so that we could put the pieces in a wheelbarrow and take them to the beach. We didn't break a single window, and the flying logs broke down only part of the garden fence, and the flying rocks made only one hole in the roof of the porch. We put everything to rights, and felt virtuous. And the lady felt grateful.

Gunpowder, like surgery, is not among the subjects taught in practical theology.

My trips to Otter's Point were more frequent and also more exciting. I mentioned Mowat's *A Whale for the Killing,* but another book of his, *The Boat Who Wouldn't Float,* entertained me more. A good deal of the brightly exaggerated narrative of that hilarious volume is about the same coastline which I navigated in an earlier and simpler time.

During my two years in Burgeo, I travelled to and from Otter's Point in a variety of ways. Once, for example, I hitch-hiked on a schooner that had stopped in at Burgeo. When the schooner reached Otter's Point it dropped a dory and put me ashore. On a number of occasions, I just borrowed a dory, a little one with a three horse power engine. And once I had a bad time in that dory.

The coasts in the Burgeo region were different from those in La Scie. They were shallow and shelving and sprinkled with treacherous "sunkers." Sunkers are rocks which in calm seas are just below the surface, but which in storms will break. On one rough trip I got out of course. Suddenly I found sunkers to the right of me, sunkers to the left of me, sunkers all around me. They may not have volleyed and thundered but they certainly scared me. And I breathed a sigh of relief when I reached clearer water.

Once in the winter when water and ice were a hazard, I took a steamer from Burgeo to La Poile 75 miles west. From there by stages I had to walk back through the woods. From La Poile to Grand Bruit to Otter's Point there were footpaths kept beaten down through the winter, and men from each place would guide me to the next. But for the last twenty-five miles from Otter's Point back to Burgeo there was no path. Almost nobody ever walked that way over land. Indeed the journey could hardly be made except in winter over snow and ice.

On this particular trip (after a Sunday at Otter's Point) two men from the island walked with me to Burgeo. We started in early morning and made the journey in a day. It was the first time that the Methodist minister in Burgeo had ever made that journey.

Having made that trip once, during my second winter I made it again by myself. However, I broke the journey by spending a night in a winter "tilt" where a family named Anderson from our church in Burgeo lived for the winter, trapping and hunting—the only family I think in that entire area.

To find one little shack in the middle of a 25 mile stretch of wild land could present some difficulty but the terrain in that locality was distinctive and I had been well instructed by men at Otter's Point. And I had a whole day before me, with every hope of fine weather.

The Andersons had no way of knowing that I was coming. But I was at ease; I knew the family well. A few months earlier their only son—"young Joe" we called him—had died of tuberculosis. The last few weeks of his life as he was coughing out his lungs, someone had to stay with him through the nights. His family did most of it, but as minister I was bound to help where possible; and I stayed with Joe through I don't know how many nights, doing such little things as I could to minister to his comfort.

In those days, we kept the windows closed after dark to ward off the night air. However, I sat in that stuffy room and survived without T.B.

I found the Anderson's tilt, indeed saw smoke coming up from it while I was quite a distance away. The Andersons, father, mother and daughter probably in her late teens, gave me a great, if surprised welcome. The next morning, with ample descriptions of the landmarks I should keep in sight, I set off again and by afternoon reached Burgeo.

I do not know if any Burgeo minister has travelled that way alone since my time; but certainly no one else had up to then. But I was still under twenty and more apt to take risks than I was after I had

An unusual sight in Burgeo harbour—a fishing and trading schooner frozen in until the spring.
The coast was usually open 12 months of the year.

In the buggy I sometimes used for transportation at Clarke's Beach.
With me, the beautiful school teacher, Winnie Goss.
Buggies were made for two.

children depending on me. "He who hath wife and family," said Francis Bacon, "hath given hostages to fortune."

As already intimated, I went to Burgeo for one year; but I stayed for two. However, it was standard practice for the Methodists to move their probationers to different places to give them experience in different circumstances. So at the end of the second year I was appointed to another charge of quite a different kind: Clarke's Beach, a pretty little village on the shores of Conception Bay.

Clarke's Beach was a change from Burgeo and La Scie. It was on the main highway, if highway is the proper word for the gravel road that wound around Conception Bay in the old settled parts of Newfoundland. It had a railway station on the branch line that had been operating for about seventy-five years. Clarke's Beach citizens could hop on the train and go on to St. John's the same day; or could turn the other way and go down the end of steel, Carbonear, only a few miles from Blackhead where we had lived in my younger years.

Clarke's Beach also had electric light and telephone, and some of the more well-to-do citizens had running water and indoor plumbing. It even had a tennis court and a little coterie of the elite who belonged to the tennis club—the minister included by courtesy. To move from Burgeo to Clarke's Beach was in essence to move from outport life to urban.

The Clarke's Beach circuit, like Burgeo, was a three point charge. On a narrow side road running about five miles down a long peninsula northward from Clarke's Beach was the historic little village of Port-de-Grave. Half way between the two places was a little cluster of houses called Bareneed—the general appearance suggested that the name was aptly given. On Sundays I normally had to preach at Port-de-Grave in the morning, Bareneed in the afternoon, and Clarke's Beach in the evening. My method of travel however was new. Along the whole way I was by the edge of the sea, but nowhere did I have to get in a boat. I looked at the water but I travelled by land.

I had a bicycle; but I did not want to be dependent on a bicycle for Sunday travel. In Newfoundland, skies often were cloudy all day—and worse. So I decided to do things in style and get a horse and buggy.

After some searching, I found that the only rig I was able to hire was a nice little buggy with the smallest of the small of Newfoundland ponies. The pony was just a little too big to keep on the mantlepiece. Sometimes when I was going down the dangerously steep hill into Port-de-Grave, I used to wonder whether the buggy was going to roll right over the pony. Yet, though its legs were short and it wasn't much at trotting, it could gallop quite fast. Sometimes I had it galloping even when driving in the buggy—a method of horsemanship not quite the approved style, especially for a minister on his way to church.

Even after I had my own rig, I sometimes travelled in more elegant style. The one person of means in Bareneed was the general storekeeper, Abe French, who became a good friend of mine. He had a second-hand touring car of some vintage ancient even in 1923. Abe would occasionally be my chauffeur. Even on the winding road to Port-de-Grave there were short spaces where we could travel up to twenty-five miles an hour. These were exciting moments, but perhaps not so exciting as tearing around a curve and finding a horse or cow lying in the roadway.

The churches at Bareneed and Port-de-Grave both had small but

79

dedicated Methodist congregations. They included, as did my congregation at Burgeo, people as fine as any I have met in my lifetime. The man I stayed with at Port-de-Grave for example, "Happy Jack" Mugford, was one of those characters who would be, for anyone who knew him, unforgettable.

Clarke's Beach, however, was the centre of most of my parishioners, and most of my work. The church there was a splendid building (as many Newfoundland churches are). It had a pipe organ and an exceptionally talented organist named Will Noseworthy, son of Clarke's Beach's most eminent citizen and the man in whose house I boarded. Not only Will but the whole Noseworthy family was musically gifted. His wife was a superb pianist with perfect pitch and his daughter, Doris, was a soprano soloist who could have been a professional.

I was not the only boarder at the Noseworthy's. With me were the two schoolteachers in the Clarke's Beach Methodist school: Bert Butt the red-headed and likeable master in the upper room and Winnie Goss the strikingly beautiful teacher of the primary room. (Alas!

Bert Butt, master of the upper room at Clarke's Beach,
with Newfoundland ponies
not much larger than the better known Newfoundland dogs.

She died of T.B. only a few years later). With Doris to make up the foursome we were a congenial group, and had a good year.

The Clarke's Beach church had more organization than the other churches in which I had worked and I got more experience in the routine of what the regular ministry would demand.

That year in Clarke's Beach completed the three which were required for me to be approved as a student for the ministry.

Before this time, I had made the shift of intent from law to the ministry. In my teens I had been interested in politics as an enthusiastic supporter on the then Premier of Newfoundland, Sir Richard Squires, one of the most dynamic leaders and one of the most brilliant men in Newfoundland history. But unfortunately he and his government became involved in charges of gross political corruption. The enquiry disillusioned me.

I came to think that I would find a better life in the ministry than in politics. I was aware that I would have to abandon one of my ambitions—to be rich. But while I would never despise riches I had a standard of values in which wealth was not essential.

At the end of my Clarke's Beach year I went to St. John's to appear in Gower Street church before a committee which examined probationers and approved or rejected them as candidates for the ministry. Quite unexpectedly, in my case, the examination—or at least my replies—struck sparks.

At the time I appeared before the committee, two other candidates whom I did not then know appeared with me. One of these was a Newfoundlander; the other a curly-haired recruit from the Methodist Church in England.

The Newfoundland student commended himself most favorably to the examiners. As to the infallibility of John Wesley's theology he had "no manner of doubt, no probable, possible shadow of doubt." In that and in every other inquiry he never struck a jarring note. He was more orthodox than the committee itself.

But the young Englishman, Ewart Cockram, and I both caused the venerable clergymen some dismay. We spoke in language in which they caught the tones of a dangerous modernism. We had been reading Harry Emerson Fosdick!

When all the questions were over the committee sent us out of the room. They passed the third man with flying colours but told Ewart and me (by now comrades in arms) to wait outside until they had time to consider our case.

81

We learned later that we got by on a narrow margin. We were saved by one member of the committee, the Rev. R. Edis Fairbairn, an Englishman who later served in the Toronto Conference. He persuaded the committee that we seemed to have in our character the seeds of redemption. So the committee called us back and, with some misgiving, gave us the necessary recommendation.

Alas for the wisdom of learned men. Our young friend in whom the committee saw the hope of the future proved as slick in other enterprises as he had been in dealing with them. In his first pastorate after ordination he lasted one year. After he had left—by popular request—the church authorities discovered that he had skilfully looted a trust fund. In less than another year he was in jail. Not long after his release he was back for another two years; he had started an import business which he operated with a certain indifference to customs duties. His further years are not recorded in church history.

On the other hand, Ewart Cockram, the curly-haired young Englishman, became in World War II the chief chaplain of the Royal Canadian Air Force. By his sensitivity, his compassion and his devotion he became for large numbers of airmen and their families the *Padre Par Excellence—Sans Peur et Sans Reproche.*

As for myself, if any of the reverend fathers of that august committee had been told that the young candidate so tainted by dangerous thoughts would in later years, in that same church, be elected Moderator of the United Church of Canada, the committee proceedings, I am afraid, would have had to record death by apoplexy.

Students for the Methodist ministry had to obtain not only recommendation to college but also approval for the college they chose. This issue rarely raised any difficulty because most of the students chose Methodist colleges in Canada. My father and my sister Millicent had both attended Mt. Allison in New Brunswick. But I considered that having lived in Methodist villages all my life, I would find a better setting for a liberal education in a metropolitan community. So I decided to go to Victoria College, Toronto. Victoria, like Mt. Allison, was a Methodist college and therefore bound to be approved.

With everything in order, I went back from St. John's to Clarke's Beach, where on July 13th, I preached my last sermon to my three congregations. Though at the time I did not know it, I was winding up my ministry in Newfoundland.

By chance it happened that my father was that summer finishing his pastorate in Grand Bank, and moving to Bay Roberts a few miles along the road running north from Clarke's Beach. So I was able to stay with my parents for the last few weeks before leaving home for the last time.

I found no work for the summer. But I was able to earn a little extra because I received enough invitations from other churches to fill in every available Sunday with summer preaching.

I am not likely to forget my final engagement. It was in Topsail, a village just outside of St. John's—the place where Jim Pratt had taken me on my first ride in an automobile. I arrived there Saturday night feeling a bit unwell. Sunday morning I knew that I had the measles—the evidence was already on my face. But I felt that it would be impossible on such short notice to get another minister. I figured that my summer sunburn would be a helpful disguise, and that, though I felt terrible, I could get through an hour. So I decided to say nothing and act as though all was well. I got through the service even if the sermon shrank a bit, went back to my room, explained my predicament to my hosts, who were kind but couldn't do much about it, and went to bed. The next morning I rose and headed for the train, and home; the measles in full flower. I went to bed and felt really sick, and apprehensive. For before the tell-tale blotches were completely gone, I got up again and, spotted or not, started off on my long journey to Toronto and a University education. Dare I say that it was a measly way to begin?

Father and mother, sitting beside the old-fashioned radio
that provided news and entertainment
in their retirement home in Carbonear.

Ruby, the best horse I ever had.
This was after I got her in top condition.
I resolved early that no farmer was going to feel
the slightest contempt for the minister or his horse.

Chapter 7

The College Crisis

*pinching pennies
and working my way
through school*

When I arrived in Toronto I went first to the home of Mrs. John Guy, who had been one of my chief parishioners in Burgeo. Her husband, who used to be the captain of a small steamer, decided to leave Newfoundland and go to Toronto to find better prospects for his family. He died suddenly en route. After bringing his body back to Burgeo for burial, the family came on together up to Toronto.

Thus, while I was landed alone in a strange big city, I moved only from one Newfoundland home to another. And for some years as I moved back and forth, the Guy home was my anchorage.

When I went to Victoria College to register I ran into trouble. I had been told that the best preparation for the ministry was Vic's Honours course in Philosophy, English and History. That was the course I decided to take. But it had stiff entrance requirements. They included Latin, which I had not taken at all, and more Mathematics and Science than I had taken in St. John's.

The registrar told me that I could overcome my handicap by going to Albert College, Belleville. Albert made a speciality of tutoring university students who had to do extra work in addition to the regular first year curriculum. My additional subjects would be Latin, Mathematics (I took Trigonometry) and Chemistry. I would have to bring these and my regular first year curriculum to the level at least of second class honours, in order that I might be admitted the next year to second year honours, Philosophy, English and History.

I had never heard of Albert College. But the registrar made it clear that Albert offered me the only way to double up on subjects without losing a year. As to extra work, I was not afraid of that. I had already learned to do a lot of extra work. So, in a few days from

*my product
was something less
than my sales pitch*

my arrival in Toronto I was on my way out to Albert College.

Thanks to the Victoria registrar, I had made a wise move. Albert had some superb teachers, and they had time for individual tutoring. Under their direction and prodding I covered more ground than I could possible have done on my own. Of course I had to work hard. But I had a room to myself and I made it a practice to get up at 5 a.m., wrap myself in a carriage blanket (the rooms were dreadfully cold early morning in winter) and get in uninterrupted hours before breakfast.

Despite my curriculum, however, I was by no means a recluse.

I spent quite a few weekends preaching in various churches in that part of old Ontario. Each visit was to me an event (for example seeing cheese made, fields harvested, or having pumpkin pie with whipped cream and maple syrup) and I made some little extra money for casual expenses. We students got the invitations to take Sunday services because Albert had long been known as a convenient source of supply preachers.

In addition to weekend diversions I took an active part in college activities, notably the debating society. I skated, and even made the rugby team, though again I had to compensate in speed for what I lacked in weight. Again, also, I thought about the calamity if I should break a bone and lose a year. But that did not inhibit me in action.

At the end of the college year I found that coming to Albert had paid off. I finished my first Arts year and I wrote and passed the exams in the extra subjects that I had lacked. And I had obtained in total a level of marks which would grant me admission to that Honours course in P.E.H. I was greatly pleased. I looked forward to the beginning of the next college year. I had no premonition that again I would be waylaid by the unexpected, and that, when I next registered at a University, it would be not in Toronto but in Halifax.

My immediate concern was to get a job for the summer—at that time, in that place, no easy task. I applied for a job mixing concrete on one of the new highways running out from Belleville toward

Kingston. At that time men with shovels did what great machines do now. However, too many others applied and I failed to get the job. At last, for lack of anything better, I got a job with a firm called the Scarborough Map Company.

I was to be an itinerant salesman for maps of Ontario, wandering, as I was sent, through various parts of the province. The maps sold for seven dollars and the salesmen got about half. I was not shown one of the maps I was selling; I was simply given a spiel to learn by heart, and from that I thought that the maps were quite magnificent. Only when I got my first consignment, for delivery to those soft-hearted individuals who had been beguiled by innocence and had signed on the dotted line, did I learn that my product was something less than my sales pitch.

I seldom sold more than two maps a day, sometimes none. At the end of the summer I had earned somewhat less than the promised minimum of seven dollars a day. But when I went to collect the money I ran into difficulties. The company refused to pay, saying that I had contracted to put in 75 days, but had put in only 74. I offered to put in another day, but they refused: the contract was finished. I went to a lawyer, Leo Macaulay, and together we visited the manager of the Map Company. He was a hard boiled customer. Out of $140 - $150 he still owed me, he settled with Macaulay for an immediate cash payment of $80. Macaulay took $20, and left me with $60.

It was not a profitable summer.

So with my summer a disaster I decided that I would have to do again what I had already done, that is exchange time for money.

I went back to Toronto and started to look for a job. For me this was a new experience, that provided some education I would not get in any class room. For days, indeed for a few weeks, I followed a tiring routine. Every day I would go downtown fairly early to look at the first newspaper to see what jobs were advertised and then try to be first at the place that looked most promising. I had bought a bicycle.

I tried the regular places, like Massey Harris, Eaton's, Simpson's and so on. On some occasions I went down to the waterfront and stood in line to see if I could get a job as a longshoreman. There were always lines of men hoping to be hired for the day. They would be called one after another until finally an official would call out, "No more." At times, I came within one or two of being called, but I never quite got the job, as scores of men behind me also did not.

I learned at least that one could be unemployed, not from laziness nor lack of ability, but simply because the job-seekers outnumbered the jobs. Since then I have always had sympathy for people looking for jobs they can't find.

But in time I did get a job. One day I was riding my bicycle out in the west of Toronto when I saw a row of houses being built. I was a good enough carpenter to do ordinary construction work. But a carpenter has to provide his own tools. A labourer does not need tools. He is just given a pick and shovel. So I went in and asked for a job as a day labourer. By good luck the contractor was just getting a squad of men to dig sewers. At that time there were no machines doing the job, just muscle power. So I was employed. My first job in Toronto was digging sewers with pick and shovel.

I had to be on the spot each morning at 8 A.M. and work till 4 P.M. with a half hour off for lunch. I was paid 50 cents an hour. This meant $4 a day, $20 a week. And as I was staying with the Guys, paying $5 a week for room and board, I was saving a little money while I looked around for something paying more.

I found nothing better; worse still, after some weeks, I was laid off from the job I had. It was then late in the fall. With almost no wasted time I got a job with the extra Christmas staff at Eaton's downtown store. For a while I sold shoes; then I sold books; then I got anchored selling ties. There I made something of a record. Toward the end of the season I sold $196 worth of ties in a day. As a dollar tie was then quite a respectable item, my record was unmatched by any other salesman in that circle.

That experience gave me an idea. I could see that almost none of the sales people really cared how much they sold or really tried to become informed in their field. I figured that if anyone went into Eaton's and gave himself to his job the way a young lawyer might work to build up a practice, he would have no difficulty in getting ahead.

If I had not been committed to the ministry I might have stayed on to seek my fortune in the Eaton's empire.

I did think of going back to Eaton's after Christmas. The temporary staff were all laid off on Christmas Eve; but we were told that after Christmas we could again apply for a job though only a few could be taken. I had no doubt that I could get taken back.

But I worked out another idea which would give me a chance of

the Sunday journey
was a triangular trek
of thirty-five miles

METHODIST

seeing more of Canada. I went down to the headquarters of the Church and I asked the Superintendent of Home Missions, Dr. Lloyd Smith, if I could have a job as a student minister somewhere out in the West, in the most difficult place they could find.

Something about my offer must have appealed to Smith because in a few days he had arranged that I would be sent immediately to a place called Forget in southern Saskatchewan.

Within a week of making my proposal I was, in the most abrupt change of pace I had yet experienced, on the train headed for that land of romance, the Canadian West.

Forget itself was a tiny village in flat prairie country that had been ranching land and should never have been ploughed. It contained a general store, a livery stable, a restaurant and not much else. Out on the edge of the little cluster of houses was a small church and a small house, now empty, which had served as a parsonage.

Though always a home mission field, Forget used to have an ordained minister. But in a current shortage of clergy, the charge had been left vacant for some time. The Forget mission field included two other preaching points, named Ossa and Coteau, which were not even villages but only sites for prairie schools, in which Sunday services were held. The Sunday journey with services for the little congregations of these three places was a triangular trek of thirty-five miles.

Travel was a problem. There were no public conveyances and no roads save concession trails dividing up the land. After half an hour of rain the black gumbo trails would be so slippery that horses would be unable to travel. There were some automobiles, mostly Model T Fords, but in the fall they were put away in barns till the roads were dry again in the spring. Even for horses, in winter the roadways were sometimes made impassible by snow.

The normal way for Forget ministers to travel—if anything could be called normal—was by horse and buggy in the summer and horse and sleigh in the winter. But I had a strong preference for riding horse-

I was afraid
to get off
lest I might never get on again

---

back. A horse could often go by himself where he could not take a buggy or sleigh. And also in the winter, when the rider reached his destination, he could go right into the barn without having to unharness the horse with half-frozen fingers.

I had done some horseback riding when I was young; but I had not been on a horse for several years. I was therefore a bit nonplussed when I arrived in Forget on Thursday and learned that it was already announced in the three places that I would be preaching on the approaching Sunday—and this without provision having been made for any means of travel.

I did not look for someone to drive me. I thought that I might as well go on my own from the start.

By enquiry, and good luck, I managed to meet a rancher, a Swede, who lived not far from Forget. Without the slightest hesitation he offered not only to lend me a saddle horse, but to throw in a saddle and bridle. He would be back with them, he told me, Saturday.

I resolved that I would not wait until Sunday morning but would go to my first stop, Ossa, on Saturday. I was told that all I had to do was to ride straight south for fifteen miles until I saw a big white house (big, that is, by prairie standards) back on a farm on the right-hand side of the road. It did not matter that the people did not know that I was coming. They would always be glad to put up the minister.

What could be more reassuring? All seemed well when my Swedish rancher arrived on Saturday with a spirited mare (half Cleveland-Bay) named Ruby. It turned out that I was to have Ruby as long as I was in Forget and that she would be the best horse I have ever ridden. But, for the moment, Ruby, though already saddled, made it clear that she had strenuous objection to being used again as a beast of burden. It took some trouble and a little help before I got on her back and we headed off for that white house at Ossa.

Remember, this was Saskatchewan in the dead of winter. The thermometer was below zero (F.). After half an hour of snow the land could be a white sea, and the road might not be discernible.

It was snowing lightly when I started. As I went it got snowier. On the whole journey I saw only a few scattered prairie shacks—all one story. When I thought that I had gone far enough, I saw one red house but no white one. After going some miles further in a steadily worsening snow storm, I decided that I had better go back to the red house and make inquiries there. I wanted to get shelter before dark, and meantime I was afraid to get off Ruby lest I might never get on again.

When I reached the red house and made enquiries, I found that it had been white. But the owner had painted it red the summer before. That was probably the only house in that region painted twice in one lifetime. Most of them had never been painted once—just as most of the farm vehicles were never put in a shed.

I put Ruby in the stable. I was chilled to the marrow; but the farm house was warm and the people were friendly, and remained my friends as long as I was in Forget. The next morning I preached at Ossa, and then after a hasty but bounteous lunch, saddled Ruby (no trouble this time) and went on my snowy way to find Coteau, which I did, preached there, and headed back to Forget for the evening service—quite a day for my first preaching assignment in Western Canada.

Riding on horseback over the Saskatchewan prairie in winter is not always a pleasant way to travel. But I made up my mind that first weekend that whenever it was humanly possible I would make my appointments and never give the people excuse to say, "It's bad going; he won't make it." I kept my resolve. I never missed a service for the winter and indeed on only a couple of occasions had a bit of a grim time. (Ironically, the one time when I didn't make it was in June, when a deluge of rain made the roads impossible for horses.)

I came to like Saskatchewan and the prairies. In some ways the prairie is like the sea. Being on the sea on a foggy day or being on the prairie in a snow storm is to be at the centre of a little bubble of visibility, beyond which the world is shut out. Wherever the traveller moves he stays on that unchanging floor, within that unchanging horizon, carrying with him his own little hemisphere of vision.

I came also to like the prairie people. Because the farm families were so isolated, they valued the times when they could get together at a church service, a neighbourhood dance, a pie social or other festival. I attended anything within range of horseback. I also made it a practice to visit farmhouses, and I did not bother too much about their denominational lineage. I was the only Protestant minister around. Church Union had been consummated the summer before; the process of merging Methodists and Presbyterians had already begun; and anyway out West denominational divisions had always been lightly marked. I was not in the least concerned with adding to church roles, but solely with establishing a religious centre to serve whom it could.

When I arrived in Forget arrangements had been made for me to stay with a family in town which happened to have suitable accommodation—perhaps the only place in town that did. The man in the family happened to be a convinced though not a belligerent atheist. However, we got along all right. But I was on the go so much, and home so uncertainly, that it was a bit of a nuisance for the woman of the house. So with the coming of spring I cleaned up the old empty parsonage and moved in there. As I often stayed overnight at a farmhouse, and sometimes was away two or even three nights in a week, batching was not an onerous task.

I travelled everywhere on horseback, and I spent a lot of time looking after Ruby. I knew the opinion of most farmers that ministers knew nothing about caring for a horse, and I determined that no farmer would ever come to church with his horse in better shape than mine. I groomed Ruby every day with curry comb and brush, and I fed her well on oats and other grains, even touching them up with molasses (plentiful in Forget to mix with poison for fighting grasshoppers). I rode her hard to keep her in condition. I soon reached the point where farmers were admiring the minister's horse, instead of the reverse.

Of course I was not without some trials. One Sunday morning in the spring, I had finished my first service and had to dash off to a nearby farmhouse for lunch. When I swung into the saddle Ruby left the ground and went heavenward in a mighty leap. By that time however I could manage a fair degree of bucking. I survived that one jump and managed to throw myself off and land on two feet. A farm hand had put a burr under the saddle, and several young lads in the know were waiting to see what would happen.

The fact that I survived, and that I knew exactly what was the trouble and went immediately for the burr, did me no harm in the eyes of the pranksters.

Another event that I remember with pleasure was an afternoon wolf hunting, that is, coyote hunting, on the prairie. With Ruby, this

My friend Bob Wilkes with the lead dogs
from the coyote hunt we went on at Forget.
Coyotes were the scourge of the farmyards.
He presented me with the skin.

time in team with a magnificent stallion, harnessed to a special sleigh built to house the wolfhounds, a young friend of mine and I had a great afternoon. The last wild run with our hounds ahead and us behind, the horses galloping full speed, the sleigh bumping and bucking over the uneven prairie and my friend somehow standing on his feet and every now and then letting out a wild halloo—that was an occasion to make fox hunting in England look tame.

In the midst of all this I had what St. Paul called the care of the churches. In addition to the preaching there were the conventional duties ranging from baptisms to funerals. I recall once having to take the funeral of a man who had died in a remote area where there was no Protestant clergyman. I rode my solitary way over the prairie twenty miles to the graveyard and twenty back, in the middle of a Saskatchewan winter.

In addition I had had enough experience from Newfoundland to know that a church, to be strong, must have some organization and play a useful part in the community. So I got Women's Associations set up in each of the three preaching areas, and in Coteau a Young People's Association. I even brought in an outside speaker for a series of Missionary Meetings to raise some contributions for the

93

work of the church beyond the local communities.

I made reports of all these things and sent them in to the Saskatchewan Conference, now not Methodist but United Church. I suggested that Forget could profit from having a regular ordained minister even though it would have to remain a Home Mission field.

By good fortune the coming of the church union with the resulting amalgamations eased the pressure for ministers. Before the conference was over I heard that a minister was available, and that he would be arriving in Forget on the first of July.

All of a sudden my Forget job was over. The congregation was as surprised as I. And I think that while we welcomed the coming of a permanent minister, my departure brought a measure of regret on both sides.

For myself I was glad that after some years without any minister at all, and a few months with an interim supply, Forget was again to get a minister regularly stationed. I knew that the alternative was nobody, for I had decided that, come September, I was going back to college to take up again my interrupted studies.

The Saskatchewan Conference not only appointed a minister to Forget, it appointed me to a new station not far from Gull Lake in the north of Saskatchewan. This was an area of thinly scattered small settlements. The mission field had four preaching points: Script, Dalton, Barrier Lake and Flagstead.

The short time that I would be there made it impossible for me to do more than maintain the summer schedule of preaching services. I got a good saddle horse, not the equal of Ruby but satisfactory, and I started again to visit the outlying farm families.

Beyond the usual routine this time I encountered one special feature of Western Canadian life: harvest time.

In those days, farmers did not have the huge combines with which in one operation they reap their wheat today. They counted it a great advance to get even threshing machines. Some of them still had steam operated outfits. With threshing machines the harvesting process was a series of operations. One of the toughest jobs of all was that of the stooker. He was the man who followed the reaping machine and stacked the cut grain into stooks, which would later be tossed into wagons and so carried to the threshing machines. As I was to learn, stooking in a field with a heavy crop was a killing job, especially on the first day out.

Each year trainloads of men went out West to work in the harvest, at wages that were then counted high. Even working for a short period, men could pay their train fare and still go back with a good nest egg. Yet for all the swarms of men that came to the prairies there were often places where farmers were desperately short of manpower.

I found myself in such a situation, and decided to make some extra money stooking. I got a job from one of the farmers I was visiting. I came to visit and the next morning as he started to mow I started to stook. It happened that he had a good crop, which made the stooking all the harder. All day I followed that horse *THOSE HORSES* and mowing machine. All day I wrestled inexpertly with those stooks. I wondered at times whether I would have to be picked up and carried home. I might have been, but for a fanatic determination that as a minister I would not be less tough than anybody else.

Despite my aching limbs I kept up to that inexorable mowing machine ahead. I got through the day. I went back the next morning. I finished that week, did my Sunday itinerary and went back to the fields again. I was not, I may say, stealing any time from my pastoral work, for at that time of the year no farmer wanted anybody around unless he could find some way to help. For the moment I was certainly a worker priest.

That was the only time I have ever worked in a western harvest. It was an interesting experience; I am a part of all that I have met. My few weeks in my new location went rapidly by. I was eagerly anticipating my return to Victoria College, but I had to make a change in my plans. Father had been ill. Letters from Claude suggested that we might not have him much longer. This was a bad blow, and I thought that I might better go back to Mt. Allison University in New Brunswick to be nearer to the rest of the family. I do not know now what particular advantage it might have been—it was almost as bad to be in New Brunswick as to be in Toronto. Either place was too far to permit casual travel to Carbonear.

However the blood is strong, and I decided to go homeward if not home. About the middle of September I packed my trunk and my valise, containing everything I possessed, and set out on the long train ride to the East.

A rare picture of my parents with all four of their sons together.
Taken during my debating visit from Dalhousie University.
Left to right: Carl, Claude, myself and Bill.

Chapter 8:

Beyond Fences

*new directions
and a taste of possibilities*

On that eastbound train I began thinking of some aspects of the situation in which I now found myself, as a member not of the Methodist Church but of the United Church of Canada.

I was greatly excited by church union. I thought that it was the most significant move within the Protestant world since the Reformation; that it was indeed the wave of the future.

During the summer I had received a calendar from Pine Hill Divinity Hall in Halifax. Pine Hill had been the Presbyterian Theological College, as Mt. Allison had been the Methodist. Now they both were colleges of the United Church.

Mt. Allison was a good college, but it was a Methodist college isolated in a little Methodist village. Pine Hill was not only a theological college, it had close links with Dalhousie University, an institution historically with a strong Presbyterian tincture.

I, the son of a Methodist minister, had spent all my life in Methodist villages. Should I get the rest of my education in a Methodist institution?

It was a narrow thing. The train was almost at Sackville when I made the decision that would change the rest of my life. I determined not to get off at my ticket's destination but to go on to Halifax, to Dalhousie and Pine Hill.

Unfortunately my trunk was checked and the train stop lacked time to get it. So I had to leave it behind and land in Halifax with only a valise. But that was a minor consideration. I knew that I would be causing more perturbation among my Methodist examiners in Newfoundland. After announcing my change from Victoria to Mt. Allison, now I was entering an institution where no Newfoundland probationer had ever before gone.

When I landed in Halifax, I took a taxi, drove up to Pine Hill and asked to see Principal Clarence Mackinnon. I told him my story, who I was, how I had landed on his doorstep, and why I wished to stay at Pine Hill residence while I attended Dalhousie University and took theological courses at Pine Hill Divinity Hall.

Dr. Mackinnon listened with great courtesy (a trait of his) and then welcomed me most warmly. I was immediately given a room. I had practically no money with me in Halifax, but that issue was never raised. Faster than I could have checked in a hotel, I was hanging up my clothes (such as they were) in a closet, and beginning a sojourn that was to last until I had graduated from both Dalhousie and Pine Hill.

Principal Mackinnon was an extraordinary man. He was among the most influential teachers I have ever met, and certainly one of those whom I would most freely call my friend. He was not an original scholar but I suspect that there were few scholars of his time who could match him, as in a church history class he could touch dead things of the past and bring them to life. More important than anything academic however, was the immeasurable impact of his character. Critics at the time used to say that all Pine Hill students became little imitations of Clarence Mackinnon. That was not true; but it was not without truth.

Pine Hill Residence, which took something over 100 boarders, was not limited to students in theology. Deliberately, it kept the gates open for university students of every faculty. In my first year for example, I roomed with a budding engineer, later with a chemist. By the time I got to theology I had a room to myself.

Because of the work I had done at Albert College I was able to enter the Dalhousie Arts course in second year. Thus I could get my B.A. in three years. I was further able to sandwich into those years some of the required theological courses. Altogether, this enabled me in five years to graduate with both a B.A. from Dalhousie and the Honours Diploma from Pine Hill.

My years at Dalhousie and Pine Hill meant a great deal to me. Perhaps the detours I had to take *en route* to college gave me an advantage. My years as teacher and probationer, my varied experiences in Newfoundland, in Ontario, and out West, my substantial apprenticeship in public speaking, and some growth of maturity as a legacy of the years, all gave something I would not have had, had I gone

it came as a stunning surprise when I was informed

from high school straight to university. Handicaps become assets.

My curriculum was not too hard to handle. I was carrying only a reasonable load, which required only a reasonable amount of diligence. Among the professors however, I did meet a superb coterie of teachers, a shining few to whom I have ever since been consciously in debt. They included James Thomson, Archie MacMechan, C.L. Bennet, George Wilson, and a peculiar star among them all, H. L. (Herbie) Stewart, from whom in my last two years I took six courses in Philosophy. Had I been able to take twelve, I would have done so. After all my contacts through all the subsequent years I still count Herbie as one of the most brilliant men I have ever met. I still unconsciously try to phrase sentences as he did; but I lack the sparkle.

Much of the education I gained from Dalhousie, however, came from outside the classrooms.

In my first year I made the debating society one of my chief interests, and was fortunate before the year was over to be chosen as one of three debaters to represent Dalhousie in a debate with St. Francis Xavier University in Antigonish. My really big break, however, came in my second year.

One of the most prestigious events then in the Canadian university year was an annual visit of the Oxford debaters. Students from Oxford University would make a nation-wide tour of Canadian universities, attracting a great deal of public attention.

The National Federation of Canadian Universities, which arranged the tours, decided that the time had come when the students who toured Canada could be not from Oxford but from Canadian universities. They decided that the first tour with Canadians as the travelling debaters should come from the East and go West. They invited three Maritime universities, Acadia, New Brunswick, and Dalhousie, each to choose one debater.

I expected the choice that year might be some student in the graduating year, or perhaps post-graduate. It came as a stunning surprise when I was informed by a committee of professors that they had chosen me.

99

almost as exciting
as it was
for Charles Dickens

I was astonished but delighted; and then I ran into trouble. The tour, after the British fashion, was to take five weeks. Although I had been selected by one group of professors, another group, the Committee on Studies and Attendance, stepped into the case. That committee said that five weeks absence was too much, and that if I went on such a tour I would not be granted credits for that year.

My day of elation was brief. I thought that the whole thing was over.

Then Clarence Mackinnon took up the cudgels on my behalf. He was wise enough to know that the experience I would get in such an enterprise would be of more benefit than anything I would get sitting in class rooms. He voiced strongly his opinion that even with five weeks absence I would be able to handle the year's studies. In the end I got a letter from the Committee on Studies saying that I was incurring too great a risk, but that if I chose to take the responsibility, they would not forbid my going.

That cross-Canada tour was for me an invigorating experience. The debates themselves were exciting encounters. We had three subjects: That sports were carried to excess in Canadian universities; That installment buying was in the best interests of the public; and That education in Canada should be national not provincial. The colleges we visited had the choice of subject and of side. So at each place we had to be prepared to take either affirmative or negative on any of the three topics. In Calgary and Victoria, which did not at that time have universities, we debated at Service Clubs.

We did well. We had a total of thirteen debates. The parliamentary debate at the University of Toronto made no judgement as to who won or lost. Of the other twelve we lost two and won ten.

But, as Clarence Mackinnon knew, the debates themselves were not all. For myself the tour was a tremendous experience. Here was I only three years up from Burgeo and Clarke's Beach, speaking (sometimes to large audiences) in the great cities of Canada from Atlantic to Pacific. Even in the University of Montreal, which we took on as well as McGill and which was one of the two places where we lost (on split decisions by the judges), the report on the front page of the Montreal *Star* next morning said that despite the decision "it was conceded that the most fluent and ablest speaker of the evening was Mr. Howse of Dalhousie University." This appeared the next day in the Halifax papers. The experience for me was almost as exciting as it was for Charles Dickens when he first saw his name in print. Montreal!

In addition to our experiences on the platform, we were everywhere most hospitably received and went through a steady succession of receptions in our honour. The reception in Victoria was given by the Lieutenant Governor at Government House. At Victoria, also, we were interviewed by Pathe News and featured on the newsreels of Canada. After I got back to Halifax I was able to attend a movie (where many other Dalhousie people were present) and see myself in the "news of the Week." In those days that was something.

Another debate the next year was almost as exciting. The Methodist College Literary Institute, of St. John's, Newfoundland, a debating society almost a hundred years old, invited Dalhousie University to send a debating team for a public debate in St. John's. The Newfoundland papers gave the event enormous publicity and the debate was held in a packed auditorium, with my parents among the audience. I was delighted to be one of that team and to make my first return to St. John's since I had met my committee in Gower Street Church.

In addition to taking part in debates I was active in the Sodales, the Debating Society, and for a year was President. During that year I inaugurated, in Nova Scotia, university debating over radio. I conducted the debates over CHNS from the Lord Nelson Hotel. (First topic: Should we pity our grandchildren?) I also arranged some parliamentary debates and invited well known Nova Scotians to lead off. All in all we had a program more varied than Dalhousie had known up to that time.

I also did a considerable amount of writing for the Dalhousie *Gazette,* and was at different times its news editor and its associate editor. I still have among my papers the first front page I ever measured and arranged and set up by myself.

As an extra, I gave some time to dramatics and in my final year took the leading part in a play put on in Nelson Hall, downtown Halifax (Halifax *Herald*: "Outstanding was the work of Ernest Howse as 'Colonel Robert Rudd'").

Supplementing all these I had some positions to which I was elected, occasionally without any enthusiasm of my own. I was Secretary-Treasurer of the Arts and Sciences Society, Secretary of the Literary Club, President of the Sociology Club, and I had some other jobs which now I do not even remember. During my last two years at Pine Hill I was one of the Editors of the Pine Hill *Messenger*. And in my graduating year at Dalhousie I was elected Valedictorian.

I did not forget my studies. I was able to carry something of an extra load, especially the intense preparation for debates, because I kept up the habit acquired at Albert College of rising early and getting in uninterrupted study before breakfast.

Counting my debating tours, the variety of activities to which I was introduced, and the influence of a small number of exceptionally fine teachers, I found my years at Dalhousie rich. I never regretted that I changed my mind on the train and went on to Pine Hill. I graduated in Arts in 1929 and in Theology in 1931.

Chapter 9:

Fields Far and Near

bucking horses
and prairie pastorates

My university years were not limited to the college terms. There were also the summers, and they too provided me with some rich experiences. I rounded out my training for the ministry by spending my summers on mission fields. The places to which I went, especially my one last summer in Saskatchewan, all brought something unexpected and unique.

For my first summer, I stayed in Nova Scotia and went to Scot's Bay, a pleasant fishing village over the North Mountain from Kentville. On Sundays I had to preach also in two other places along the North Mountain: Arlington and Baxter's Harbour. That involved a drive of something like ten miles along hilly roads. And that in turn led to the happiest parts of my summer's experience.

Once again, I had to get a pony. By great good luck I got one of the best race horses in Nova Scotia at the time. A farmer named Burbage in Kentville used both to breed horses and race them. He had one mare, as well bred as anything he had ever owned but which in her first season on the track had been a disappointment. She was just a good race horse, not a record breaker. Burbage wanted to try her again next season, but in the summer was too busy to give her exercise. I was able to persuade him that she would be safe in my care. He lent her to me with a light buggy not much heavier than a regulation sulky.

I had a fair amount of spare time that summer and I spent most of it with that mare. She was high strung and often gave me quite a battle to get her hitched to that sulky and to get myself on board and in control before she started down the road. The whole village soon knew that mare. They would stand by the road or watch out the windows to see me tearing by. We made such time as horse and buggy had never before made on the Scot's Bay road. She was the only thoroughbred I ever got to handle. But when I gave her back at the end of summer she was certainly in prime condition, and Burbage was greatly pleased.

A postscript. In the summer of 1963 I went to Nova Scotia to give a series of addresses at Berwick Summer Camp—a century old institution without parallel in Canada. One day I decided to drive down to Scot's Bay to look up some of the people who had been so good to me many years before. So my wife and I set off in search of the past. At Scot's Bay, alas, because of the widening of the road and the decline of population, almost nothing I had known was left, save the little corner store. I went in and gave my name to a girl behind the counter. She showed no recognition, but when I told her I had come from Berwick Camp, she said, "Oh. I'll get Mrs. Steele."

Mrs. Steele rushed out, recognized me and said, "I saw your picture in the Halifax paper last night. I always remembered you, and that sorrel mare."

While we were talking an old man came in. Mrs. Steele called him and said, "This is Mr. Howse. You remember, he used to be a minister here."

The old man shook his head; the name didn't resurrect anything. She said, "Don't you remember that sorrel mare?"

The old man turned to me, his eyes lit up, and he said, "Oh, Yes."

Over thirty years had passed since I had been a student minister in that place; and a man who could not remember me could remember my sorrel mare.

My second summer was in a setting vastly different from Scot's Bay. I volunteered again to go out to the western provinces. I was appointed to a little settlement called Richmond.

I knew nothing about Richmond; this was not surprising because Richmond did not exist six months before. It was a brand new settlement at the end of a new spur line of railway. Until the railway came, its terminal an old box car minus the wheels set down by the side of the track, not a single dwelling had stood where Richmond had since been built. When I arrived that prairie metropolis had a couple of grain elevators, a general store, a hardware store, a livery stable and a scattering of one storey houses. But everything was new. Not one building except that boxcar station had been touched with a paint brush.

The place where I was appointed to stay was a little two room shack, as new as all the others. One room was the kitchen, the post office, and common room for the community. The man living there, I forget his name now, was postmaster, insurance agent, butcher and according to a sign in the corner, agent for tombstones—though I am not sure that there was as yet any necessity for a tombstone, or that there was even a corner of land set aside for a graveyard.

The other half of the shack, still not quite finished, was the bedroom. I might call it the suite of bedrooms. A rope was stretched across the middle of the room, and a blanket was hung on the rope. You dropped the blanket and that was the partition. The man and his wife were allotted one side; and the hired man and any other guests on the other. Fortunately the hired man had recently gone on his way; and the man's wife was in the hospital in Maple Creek, where she was to remain for the next six weeks. I suspect that had it not been for her misfortune I might not have had a place.

The man quickly made it clear that he expected me to prove my worth by being the chief cook and bottle washer. So, trying like St. Paul to be all things to all men, I pitched in and did the best I could.

Fifteen miles away was a second place, aptly called Surprise, which consisted of a cross roads where a farmer kept the post office. Because of the two places, my first task was the familiar one of getting a horse, and somewhere scrounging a saddle and bridle. Again I

My Montana cow pony at Richmond.
With the bridle hanging like this, she would stay put.
Without the bridle, "for ways that are dark and tricks that are vain..."
but she was a great cow pony.

was lucky. For a consideration of ten dollars, a farmer sold me a vintage Montana cow-pony.

Bridled and saddled she was a remarkably good cowpony. With the reins dropped to the ground she would stay as if tied to a post, and on the go she would answer to the touch of a knee. But one day, unfortunately, I let her get away in the nude. I picked up the bridle and went after her. And that was the beginning of troubles. At any time I could walk up to within twenty feet of her. But at that point she kept the biblical injunction, "Thus far shalt thou come and no farther." That pony kept to her convictions. I spent almost a whole day moving on and on, near enough to that pony to talk to her (which I sometimes did in language tinctured with the theological). In that new area there were no fences. And I did not want to have my horse tramping through some farmer's already poor crops.

I covered I figured about twenty miles with that pony. Whenever I tried to close in, she led me on just far enough and fast enough to keep out of reach. Yet when she graciously agreed to be caught, she was as fine a saddle pony as you would want.

The area in which those two tiny settlements, Richmond and Surprise, were situated, was, I soon found out, one where I could not be of much use. Practically all the new settlers were Ukrainian or German. I had arrived there early in May, and by June, the time of the annual United Church Conference having jurisdiction over that area, I had sent an urgent letter saying that it was useless to send anyone there who spoke only English.

I must have made my case, because I received a reply saying that for the rest of the summer I was to go to Piapot—a little railway town not far from Swift Current. Piapot was tiny but long-established. It had once been the centre of large cattle ranches and the surrounding area was still so thinly populated that I had to keep circulating through seven preaching points, taking three services a Sunday. Piapot, where I lived, was the one constant weekly place of worship.

Such a schedule made it impossible for me, in a three month's stint, to do more than take the Sunday services and during the week to visit some of the more loyal church families. Even to do that required a great deal of travelling, and to do the travelling I had once more my old problem of getting a horse.

And once more my most exciting days of the summer were to be in the saddle.

the young preacher could ride any horse, anywhere, even Poison

By this time I almost had a *modus vivendi*. I borrowed a saddle pony in Piapot and rode out to a large ranch only a few miles south. The rancher was a Roman Catholic chap named McCarthy, and he was generous to a degree. He lent me a first class saddle pony, and also a saddle and bridle.

The pony had been saddle broken, but had not been ridden for a year or so and was a bit wild. That was to lead me into an experience of which I had no prevision.

I kept the pony in the stable of the then unused parsonage, which was still in good condition, and boarded with the lady who had before her retirement owned the general store. One morning as I got on the pony, it started to buck. I was not a good enough rider to stay on a horse with my hands free, in stampede fashion. But I was good enough so that by hanging on to the horn I could bring a pretty rough horse to order.

By chance, a man named Mercer who had taken over the store, happened to see me fighting it out with the horse. This gave him the idea of playing what he considered a good joke on the young minister. In an almost empty area about twenty miles from Piapot there was an old man named Mose Elliott. In earlier days he had been a well known rancher, and one of the notable contenders in the Maple Creek Stampede. In my time, he was over seventy. He had retired to a square mile of uneven prairie and bushland on which he kept about fifty horses. Everybody knew Mose Elliott. He was a celebrity, and, as I was to learn, a first class gentleman.

In those days in certain areas, where large ranches or farms were surrounded by barbed wire, ingenious farmers would hook up one of the wires in a home-made telephone system. Thus, by their own inter-com, they could talk across the distance to a neighbour and so on. Mose had such a telephone.

Somewhere Mercer got on to Mose's phone and told him that the young preacher from the East had boasted that he could ride any horse, anywhere. Mose took the bait. He said to Mercer, "Send him out to me."

I knew nothing about the call. Mercer simply told me that there was a fine old rancher living out in a lonely area who would be pleased to see me. I too took the bait, and one morning set off for a twenty mile ride to visit Mose.

I got there just about lunch time. During lunch time we talked mostly about horses, and then Mose said calmly, "Now, we'll get Poison." I had no idea what he wanted except that he must have a horse by that endearing name. I did not know that the horse got the name by his performance in the bucking contests at the Maple Creek stampede. We got on horseback and took off. At first we couldn't see any horses. Much of the square mile that Mose had wired in was uneven brush and the horses were in there to get away from the heat. However, we rode into the bush and shortly we saw the horses, and suddenly Mose pointed to a huge white beast and said, "There he is. There's Poison."

I thought then that I knew what we had to do. Near his stable Mose had a corral; and in the corral a squeeze. A squeeze is a narrow place between two fences where a horse can go in but cannot turn around. You drop a log behind him and then saddle him by reaching through the rails. When all is ready you open the exit, and out comes an avenging fury a la Calgary.

I knew enough about the job to help Mose get Poison into the corral. But then to my surprise Mose brought out a saddle and we proceeded to get it cinched on Poison.

I was still mystified as to what he was doing. And then, like a blinding light, it struck me. Mose expected me to ride that beast. I nearly fainted on the spot.

I was scared. I never would have got on Poison but for one thing. Though I was scared of what Poison would do to me, I was still more scared of what would happen to my stature in that area if I chickened out. So, with I hope no visible trembling, I gave my glasses to Mose, climbed over the top of the rails and dropped down on the saddle.

my spine hit his back—
I saw only a flash
of darkness

Poison came out of that squeeze with a jump that almost made me the first astronaut in Canada. He headed for the stratosphere and then came down and my spine hit his back. I saw only a flash of darkness. Then he corkscrewed and I kept going upward longer than he did. When I hit the ground, which was fortunately sandy and soft, I got up gingerly, shook myself and found happily that I had no broken bones.

Then Mose came along with his comforting word. He just said casually, "We can try again."

Three times that afternoon I got on that horse and three times I was tossed ignominiously to the dust. I was battered and bruised, my nose was bleeding and my white shirt was stained with red. But when all was over I had Mose as a friend for life.

He twigged as to what the set up had been. So when the next morning, tender from head to foot, I started back for Piapot, Mose himself got in the act. He got on his phone and told Mercer the most hair-raising tale of how I could ride that beast. When I was nearing Piapot I saw half a dozen small boys coming out on the road toward me and when I got near they started to wave their hands. The legend had begun that I could ride Poison.

As legends do, this legend lived on. One of those boys who came out to cheer my return was a son of Mercer's. He became a minister and long years later he became one of my successors in Westminster Church, Winnipeg. On the night of his induction he told the congregation that the first time he heard of Westminster Church was when he learned that a former minister of theirs had been the young probationer so many years before who had ridden Poison.

That year when I was down to Berwick Camp, 1963, a young theological student who had spent the previous summer out in the Peace River district told about visiting a family who had built themselves a shack and were starting to farm in a new area. The lady came to him with a copy of the latest *Observer* which happened to have a photograph of me. The lady pointed to my picture and said, "That's the man who rode Poison." The year I rode Poison was 1928; the year the lady spoke to the student was 1962. What other effort of mine has been remembered so long?

After my first visit to Mose I went back frequently. We shared some marvellous experiences. One time I joined with him to harness a team of half broken horses, and set off on a forty mile jaunt to the Maple Creek Stampede for Mose's last entry in the chuck wagon

109

we found a car,
a vehicle
seized from a bootlegger

race. But one item cannot be omitted.

About ten years later when I was a minister in Westminster Church, Winnipeg, I came home one night and turned on the radio to hear the late night news. I was in time only for the last story. The words ran like this: "An old rancher named Mose Elliott was found murdered in his cabin today." The news went on to say that Mose was alone when a stranger arrived. The stranger, it turned out, had heard a rumor that Mose in his earlier days had found gold. He murdered Mose and then almost took the shack to pieces, but of course found no gold. About a week later he was arrested in Montreal and later, I think, was hanged. It was bitter news to me. There are few people for whom I had warmer affection than for that old rancher.

That summer in Piapot was my last summer in Saskatchewan, and my last in the West until I came back from California in 1935 to be minister of Westminster United Church, Winnipeg.

The next summer, 1929, the year I graduated from Dalhousie, I went only to Rockingham, a little village just outside Halifax, now absorbed in the expanding city. When I was back in Halifax in November 1978 for the 100th anniversary of Pine Hill I got a friend to drive me out to Rockingham. I would not have known the place any more than if I had never been there before. In 1929 it was a delightful summer resort with tennis and swimming, and with some delightfully congenial families.

It was at Rockingham that I first tried out an experiment which in later years I developed considerably. I began to give sermons based on the great stories in literature. It was in effect an extension of the sermons in Burgeo based on the great stories in the Bible.

In Rockingham I did not need a horse and the pattern of my days was different. I would have been sad, had I foreseen that I would never again ride horseback.

The following summer, 1930, I also stayed in Nova Scotia. I went to a delightful place called Clam Harbour. The clams were incredibly plentiful; I went to some clam bakes never matched since. It also had a marvellous beach about a mile long on which you could drive cars at high speed. It was in Clam Harbour that I got my first car—mine, that is, in a manner of speaking.

I had to conduct Sunday services not only at Clam Harbour but at Ship Harbour, Owl's Head, Oyster Ponds and occasionally at Pleasant Point and Head of Jeddore. I was not only supposed to preach in these places on Sunday but also to keep in touch with their church affairs throughout the week. My supervising minister was a most friendly chap named George Beck. I explained to him that I could do a much better job keeping in touch with these various places if I had a car, instead of a bicycle. Somewhere Beck managed to raise the sum of $250 and with that capital we went looking for a suitable car for the Clam Harbour probationer. We found such a car. It had been a vehicle seized from a bootlegger. Our bid? $250.00. It was a Chevrolet of the year 1927 and was the first car I ever had.

The car had its deficiencies. The back seat was lacking. It had been taken out by the bootleggers to give space for a large pile of broken bottles. Tires in the twenties were by present standards flimsy, and it had been the pleasant custom of the previous owner to scatter glass along the way at any time when intrusive policemen were pressing him too hard. I got rid of the glass but still lacked the seat. For the summer I had to do with an assortment of borrowed cushions. One consequence was that I could not take older people, but the young folk did all right.

Fortunately the running gear was in topnotch condition and that battered little Chev added much pleasure to my summer in Clam Harbour.

The next summer, 1931, was my final summer on a student mission field. Actually I was by then a fullfledged minister. In June I had graduated from Pine Hill and had been ordained by the Maritime Conference. At that time I already knew the unexpected development that I would be able to go in September to Union Theological Seminary, New York. So as an interim engagement I went to a student charge at Grand Bay on the Saint John River just a few miles outside the city of Saint John, New Brunswick. Grand Bay was a delightful summer resort and I had a pleasant time before a new adventure and a strenuous year.

Esther Lilian Black
in 1932, before our marriage.

Chapter 10:

New York

*intellectual giants
and student struggles*

How it came about that I was able to go on without delay to New York, and after that to Scotland, requires a bit of explanation.

During my years in Halifax I had come increasingly to the conviction that I must somehow go on to post-graduate education. My first choice for further study was Union Theological Seminary, New York, then the leading Protestant seminary in the world. I wanted in particular to know two of its faculty, Reinhold Niebuhr and Harry Emerson Fosdick. My problem was the one I always had: money. I had managed to get through my five Halifax years without even being in debt—though I once had been down to a total of one dollar and eighty-seven cents. Today when the value of money has so radically changed, it is enlightening to recall that my rate of pay on these summer mission fields, my bread and butter income, was $15.00 a week. The utmost I could hope to earn on a summer field would hardly reach $300. And there were few possibilities to augment that meagre total by extra work, as I did stooking wheat in Saskatchewan.

In Halifax, as I got better known, I did get a number of preaching engagements. In my last year I filled in for several weeks at First United in Truro, then one of the largest congregations in Nova Scotia.

I made considerably more, however, as agent for Remington portable typewriters. In Pine Hill residence, typewriters were just coming into popular use among students. When I went there typewriters were few; when I left they were clattering in every part of the building, most of them bought from me ($75—$5 down and $5 a month). In one unequalled term I sold nineteen before Christmas.

Even so, the only factor that kept me solvent was Pine Hill's in-

113

world famous scholars
who had just
been names in books

---

credibly low rates. Theological students, even while in arts, were charged only $135 a year for room and board. And we had facilities for doing our own laundry. Thus it came about that I left Pine Hill with a bank account, resting at something like four hundred dollars.

Clearly that was not enough for me even to think about going to New York for a post-graduate year. I began to turn over my mind what I could do about the matter.

I sent for a Union calendar and, on looking through it, I discovered that there was a Preaching Fellowship, which by its terms was not limited to American students but open to applicants on a basis of scholarship, public speaking, general proficiency and other qualifications. The fellowship amounted to $650.00 plus a room for the year. It looked inviting.

I prepared an application. I had to get a transcript of marks; but, more importantly I had to get testimonial letters. I went to see Clarence Mackinnon, Herbie Stewart, James Thompson and the President of Dalhousie himself. They were all so willing to help that the glowing terms with which they commended me to Union Seminary reflected more their good will than any exact assessment of my abilities.

However, I put everything together, sent it off, and in a short time I was notified that I had been granted that Preaching Fellowship.

By co-incidence beyond my deserving I had in the meantime won another scholarship without any initiative whatever on my part. Pine Hill had a travelling scholarship of $1,000.00 given once every five years and open to any student within that period. I knew about the scholarship but had not the slightest idea that I was within reach of it. To my astonishment, just about the time I got word from Union that I had been granted their Preaching Fellowship, it was whispered to me that on graduation I would likely get that five-year Pine Hill award.

If I had known that I would get the Pine Hill travelling scholarship, I probably would not have bothered to apply for the one at Union. Suddenly, as if by the wave of a wand, I found that the doors

114

were open for me to manage both a Master's degree at Union and a Ph.D. at Edinburgh. The margins of money were no skimpier than those I had contended with through all the years past. I did not have enough to get me through. But I had enough to get me started. And with that I was ready to go.

It would be hard for me to convey the feeling of excitement and privilege that came to me as I began my year at Union. Suddenly world-famous scholars who had just been names in books began to loom up as persons and teachers and in time, some of them, as friends. Unfortunately I was not able to get in any class taught by Reinhold Niebuhr. By the time I applied his classes were already crowded. I got into only one by Fosdick, and only one seminar by John Baillie. I did however get into classes with other celebrated figures such as Henry Sloane Coffin, Union's President. And James Moffatt, famous translator of the Bible, was one of my tutors in writing my Master's thesis.

What I got from Union, however, was not limited to the class room. Reinhold Niebuhr, for example, used to have frequent "open house" affairs for students. I always attended them. His apartment used to be packed—students sitting not only on the chairs but on the floor, filling up, it seemed, every square inch. There was no program, but the excitement began as the students began to ask questions. Niebuhr's knowledge was encyclopedic in many fields, and none of us who attended his parties will ever forget them. In subsequent years I met Niebuhr in quite a few places and occasions.

James Moffatt also kept remarkable contact with students. On Sunday afternoons the Moffatts held open house for students of the British Commonwealth. Moffatt was another extraordinary man. Famous in particular for his new translation of the Bible, Moffatt in several fields ranked with the finest scholars in the world and his output of scholarly volumes was enormous. But his knowledge ran into far different fields. He was an authority on both church music and light opera. He was an expert on fly-fishing, and also on gardening, particularly the cultivation of roses. What seems still more amazing, he was said to be one of the best authorities in the United States on baseball and had few to match him in the ability to rattle off the records of any given team in any given time. He had given close study to the craft of the detective novel, and himself wrote one who-dun-it *A Tangled Web*.

Moffatt never seemed in a hurry, and always had time out for fun—including frequent afternoons at baseball games. During my Union year I had an evening with Moffatt at "The Mikado," and another at the Barnum and Bailey Circus, and some trips with him wandering through second hand bookstores—an education in itself.

Curiously, Moffatt was a poor speaker. He was invited everywhere—once. But in the days before sound systems he was often inaudible beyond the first few rows.

He told me that once he was invited to a large conference in one of the southern cities and when he arrived he saw in the leading newspaper the impressive headline: "Author of Bible to appear in city."

Harry Emerson Fosdick was another teacher whom I got to know. He was the one with whom I kept most in contact after I left Union. Time and again throughout the subsequent years I exchanged letters with him. He wrote me a cordial letter when I went first to the Middle East. He knew a great deal about the Middle East and had close connections with a number of teachers in colleges there. He commended the work I was doing.

He also, I am sure, was the one who arranged an event by which I was greatly flattered. In the year he was retiring from the Riverside Church, the summer preachers were noted as men who might possibly be his successor. I was then in Winnipeg, and was greatly surprised to be invited to take a Sunday service at Riverside. There was, I knew, not the slightest chance that I would be selected as the successor to the most famous preacher in the Protestant world. But even to be invited to Riverside that summer pleased me as much as it astonished me. When I preached there, on that first Sunday in August, 1946, the huge, cathedral-like church was crowded—not because of me, but rather because in those years Riverside was always crowded.

Outside the round of college and professors, my Union year was made notable by attendance at the theatre and the opera. This was an opening into a new world. When I went to New York in 1931 the world was sinking into the Great Depression. Theatres often could not fill their seats. They hit upon the device of sending to the colleges, at the last moment, free tickets for students. They counted it better, even if no money were coming in, to have the seats filled rather than empty. At that time the front seats in a good theatre cost three dollars. For that money you could see the foremost theatrical attractions of the time. For me it seemed that spending three dollars

I can say I have played Julius Caesar off-Broadway

(six dollars with a companion) to see a show was a mark of either substantial wealth or irresponsible extravagance. Few times in my life have I felt as wealthy as I did the first time that I walked down the aisle of a Broadway theatre with a California girl (of whom I will say more later) for a date and with six dollars worth of tickets in my hand, to see the opening of a new play. Having started at a nickel movie house in St. John's, and having in that city progressed to a point where I once spent seventy-five cents to see a chorus line, I became in New York comparatively a sophisticate. During the year I must have seen a couple of dozen plays—not all of them free, not all of them on Broadway. Some of the best, including Eugene O'Neill's *Mourning Becomes Electra,* I saw at smaller theatres in cheaper areas.

Far-fetched though it may seem, I myself once appeared on a New York stage. Some social workers, dealing with the swarms of the Depression unemployed, hit upon the idea of giving free entertainment in some unused theatres. An item planned for one evening was the presentation of a scene from Shakespeare's *Julius Caesar.* All the actors were students, some of them drama students. I played Cassius. (He had a lean and hungry look, and I was then more fitted for the part than I am today.) Hence, by stretching the truth almost to infinity but without telling an undiluted lie, I can say that I have played in *Julius Caesar* in an off-Broadway theatre in New York.

Beyond the academic field we had some adventitious social contacts. Mrs. Andrew Carnegie gave a Christmas party for British Commonwealth students, with presents, by name, for every guest. She was then in her nineties, but active and sprightly and still in the famous old house Andrew had built on Fifth Avenue, with the organ on which he used to play the gospel hymns he had learned in his youth. Another time I was at a party at the house of Cleveland Dodge, and sat on the sofa where President Woodrow Wilson had first sketched out his ten points for peace.

Most important of all extras was the fact that next door to Union

Seminary was International House, of which I became a member. International House provided the opportunity of meeting with students, most of them bright students, from all over the world. An outstanding feature of its program was a regular Sunday evening dinner, followed by a concert given by the students of some national group. The rest of us sat down at random at round tables and introduced one another as we were: black, white, yellow and brown. For one just seven years out of Newfoundland it was mind-stretching.

Students from far away lands were not the only ones in the International House roster. Each year a limited number of American students were scattered among groups. One of the first American students that I met was an attractive and intelligent girl named Esther Black, from Pasadena, California. To that event I shall have to return.

My year at Union passed all too quickly. I took all the classes I could and wrote a thesis on the 18th Century English Deists. My advisers and examiners in this were John Baillie and James Moffatt. Beside the thesis, if my memory is right, I got an A in six out of seven courses. At graduation I was awarded the degree of Master of Sacred Theology (S.T.M.). The acronym was said by the irreverent to stand for "Saturday Till Monday"—the only time a minister would have to work.

My plan to go to Scotland the following year left me with a free period from May to September—the first time in my life that I had had such unbroken free time. But depression times were so desperate that I knew that I had little chance of getting casual employment, either in Canada or Newfoundland.

Earlier I had written to the United Church Superintendent of Home Missions saying that if the church would send me to some place in the West in the worst extremity of drought and depression, I would work for no salary and live on whatever the families there lived on, if the church would merely pay my way out and back. I got a reply saying that the student supply program had been reduced and that there was no provision for such an offer. I thought the response typically bureaucratic; but at any rate I was left with free time. I planned to go home and spend that time with my parents in Newfoundland. The last time I had seen them was at that debate in St. John's.

Then, with a suddenness characteristic of my experience, I was confronted with an entirely new and unexpected possibility. I would

118

the trip was
suggested
by the young lady

still go home; but I would go from New York to Newfoundland by way of California and Vancouver, with a couple of weeks in Pasadena. Incredible as it now seems, I found that I could with Depression specials, buy an excursion ticket, coach class, from New York to Los Angeles to Vancouver to Montreal for $189.00. And with another equally low rate I could go by steamer on a four day sea voyage from Montreal to St. John's.

I could handle that.

I had not done too badly during my year at Union. I had managed in various ways—such as serving as a paid usher—to supplement my scholarship funds. In particular I had got a job which covered my biggest expense—food. I washed dishes after breakfast in the Refectory at Union: no wages but free meals, of whatever was left.

The job was exhausting. I worked in a little room where the dirty dishes came in on a moving belt on one side, passed through a hot dishwashing machine and went out, dried by their own heat in racks on which I had stacked them. The system was designed for two men; but because of the Depression, one man worked alone, and for breakfast he had to work madly in steaming heat for about an hour and a half. Whatever meals I ate, I earned. But one way and another I ended my year in New York with more money than I had when I went there. I could take that California excursion.

The trip was suggested by the young lady already mentioned, Esther Black from Pasadena, an International House student taking her master's degree at Columbia University. In those distant days, when the population of California was relatively small and its natural beauties unspoiled, California really was a wonderland. And it had few more enthusiastic boosters than Esther. She lived with a deep conviction that anyone who had not seen California had not yet been born.

She gave me a warm invitation to stop off in California where she could arrange a grand tour of the glories of her spectacular homeland. As soon as I had figured that I could manage the finances

119

On our trip across the continent from New York to Pasadena.
We detoured to the Grand Canyon,
where once again I ended up in a saddle.

I gladly accepted the invitation. Further, because we ended our university year at the same time, I was able to take the New York to Pasadena portion of my journey while she was returning home. And, because she knew the best routes to take, we did not go directly to Pasadena but took a spur line to the Grand Canyon of Arizona, that unique splendor of nature, beyond description but unforgettable. To go down a mile to the bottom of the Canyon and watch all through the day the constantly changing panorama of grandeur is an experience to brighten a lifetime.

In 1952 I went down the Grand Canyon again, this time with my sons, David and George. When we were almost to the bottom, a long spell of drought broke in a tremendous thunder storm and deluge of rain. In a matter of minutes water, like that which had carved the Grand Canyon, was streaming in torrents down the pathways along which we had to return. Our tour guides hustled us as fast as they could back to the top, but even so, in one place our trail was such a foamy river that they had great difficulty in getting a lead mule to plough through so that the others would follow.

After our day at the Grand Canyon, Esther and I returned to the transcontinental line and went on to Pasadena. During the next two weeks or so I saw an astonishing amount of California: Yosemite Park, the Sequoias, San Diego Park, and on to Mexico, the Hollywood Bowl for a concert under the stars .... I probably saw more of California than some people who lived there.

The trip had a consequence which I could not at the time foresee. Esther and her family were members of the Pasadena Presbyterian Church; her father was the business manager. The minister, Dr. Robert Freeman, was one of the outstanding preachers of the time and a man of great influence in church and civic affairs. While I was in Pasadena, Dr. Freeman invited me to be the preacher for two Sundays of his summer vacation. (I think someone dropped out at the last moment.)

I had no idea that less than two years later that contact would lead to an invitation to become the minister of another prestigious California church, the Presbyterian Church of neighbouring Beverly Hills, then the residential centre of many of the leading figures in the movies.

Having enjoyed my California stay, I set out on my long journey back to Carbonear, Newfoundland.

The train journey from Pasadena to Vancouver and then from Vancouver to Montreal was in itself a memorable experience. The scenery up the Pacific Coast was magnificent. And I had one more chance of riding through the incomparable Canadian Rockies.

I spent altogether six nights on the train. Each night, by means of a strategy I used for many years, I had a berth. I would buy only a coach ticket. Then at 11 P.M. I would ask the conductor for an upper berth. Provided one was empty, the conductor would sell a night's use of an upper for $1.50. In those depression days the trains were never crowded.

In Montreal, I switched from land to sea. Before airplanes took the burden of travel, at least two passenger steamers a week sailed from Montreal to St. John's. That was a voyage of four days which I enjoyed immensely.

I went to Carbonear where my father and mother were living in retirement. They were then in a rented house; but in a later summer my brothers, Claude, Carl and Bill, all unable for a while to get jobs, applied their time by building a new house, which was attractive, well designed and a great improvement on the rented one. In that

121

to marry an
aboriginal
from the wilds of Newfoundland

house our parents lived in comfort until my father died and my mother came to Canada, spending her last days with my brother Carl.

That summer in Carbonear, 1932, was the first in which I was unable to get any work whatever. The only money I earned came from the scanty returns of summer preaching. I was one Sunday each in Cochrane Street, George Street, and Gower Street, all in St. John's. The trips to the city at least provided some diversion, and enabled me to visit old friends.

Whatever the doldrums of normal enterprise, the summer brought a radical transformation in my plans for Edinburgh. I had not seriously thought of being married until I was through university. For this there was one cogent reason. I had no way whatever of undertaking the support of a wife. I had calculated, as was then the normal pattern, on finishing my education before taking on the responsibilities of marriage.

However, during the summer Esther's parents had, I suspect, come to the conclusion that for her to marry an aboriginal from the wilds of Newfoundland was not necessarily the calamity that it seemed on first thought. At any rate her father intimated that he could put up the money necessary for her to go to Scotland. He further made arrangements by which she could have a modest income while she was there. In addition he arranged that when I arrived in New York, on the first lap of my journey to Scotland, I would have awaiting me there a return ticket to Pasadena. Even such a moderate difference in financial resource made it seem possible to go to Scotland with a wife.

When I told my parents that now I would be going to Edinburgh by way of Pasadena they were greatly astonished. I must have seemed an erratic young man. I suspect that they had some doubts about my capacity to take responsibility for so momentous a choice. And in California, where many of Esther's friends knew no more about me than my friends knew of her, the sudden tidings that she was to marry a native of Newfoundland must have been received with the greatest misgiving.

In Carbonear, I was nicely insulated from the whirl of showers and parties and wedding events. But in the month from the time the engagement had been announced to the wedding day itself, Esther and her family lived in a chain of social affairs. I arrived with but one day to spare before the colourful wedding in Pasadena Presbyterian Church. And with one day of rest after the wedding, we set out by transcontinental train on the first lap of our honeymoon trip across the Atlantic.

Unless one looks at a globe it is not readily apparent that a traveller from New York to Great Britain is almost half way through the journey when he passes Cape Race, the south-eastern corner of Newfoundland. As we were passing that landmark I realized how near we were to Carbonear and my parents. I went up to the radio room and asked the operator to send a telegram to my father and mother. It was brief, for of course we had to save money, but it came as a surprise when our telegram arrived with this brief message:

"Passing Cape Race. All well."

With the lands of our birth behind us and another world ahead, this was the final verdict: All well.

Ernest M. Howse and Esther L. Black
September 17, 1932

Chapter 11:

Scotland

*expanding my universe
and earning a Ph.D.*

We landed in Scotland (September 1932) when the Depression was world wide; but Britain had suffered even more than America. On our first day in Edinburgh having our first lunch in a little restaurant on beautiful and romantic Princes Street, I picked up a newspaper and read that in the Highlands sheep were selling at a shilling apiece—lower than at any time since the 18th century.

A few days later, I read that a ship coming from California with a cargo of oranges, steamed out of the harbour, still loaded, and dumped the whole consignment into the sea. Meanwhile in Britain multitudes of men, women and children were almost literally starving. But in the crazy economics of the day, destroying food seemed to be the way to keep prices high and bring back good times.

Fortunately the economic situation, just as it made little difference to the weather, also made little difference to the beauty of English and Scottish scenery or the fascination of their historic places. Nor did it make such a difference to my gruelling program of research for a Ph.D.

I had chosen to take my degree in the field of History—the most inclusive of all studies—but it took me some time to find a clearly defined field which would satisfy the University authorities as being a proper subject of enquiry for a doctoral thesis.

I had been reading for about three months in the general field of social reform in England in the 18th and 19th centuries when my chief advisor, Dr. Hugh Watt of New College, suggested to me that no one had done a definitive study of "The Clapham Sect." That title did not designate a religious denomination. It was a nickname given to an extraordinary group of men who at the turn of the 19th century gathered around William Wilberforce, the great parliamentary orator who brought about the abolition of slavery, and who together had an impact upon social reform unmatched by any other parliamentary coterie in English history.

I immediately began to look into that story, and I soon chose "The Clapham Sect" as the subject of my dissertation.

I was exceedingly fortunate to have found such a theme. With superb direction from my tutors and a great deal of help from a number of outside scholars, I was able to produce a study which is still the authoritative work in its field.

At the University of Edinburgh, Ph.D. theses had to be approved by three examiners, two from the university and one from outside. I learned that my third examiner was the eminent English historian, G.M. Trevelyan, and that he had recommended publication of the thesis. Shortly afterward I did make enquiry of an English publisher, Allen and Unwin, to see if publication would be possible. Without even reading the book they replied, with great courtesy, that a Ph.D. thesis would not likely be a marketable product. It was not till twenty years later, after Canadian historian A.R.M. Lower happened to read the manuscript and urge its publication, that the University of Toronto, together now with Allen and Unwin, put the book in print. It came on the market in Canada in 1952, in England in 1953.

The small Canadian edition soon sold out; but in England the book kept its modest place on the market year after year. It was chosen and remained a "set book" for the "Open University." In the 1970s, it was reprinted three times and as late as 1979 sold a total of 921 copies (100 American sales, 37 other exports). I doubt if any other Ph.D. thesis in my generation has kept a place on the open market for close to thirty years.

I began my research in Edinburgh at the National Library of Scotland, one of the four institutions to which by law the publisher of every book printed in the British Isles has to present copies. The library had a great deal of material besides books: papers, pamphlets, letters and memorabilia of all sorts. I soon learned the techniques of tracing down relevant books and documents by following reference after reference after reference. In my completed thesis I listed some seventeen pages of bibliography. But these were only the more important sources which might be helpful to readers interested in the field. Behind these were an enormous number of books and manuscripts through which I searched, and by which I

126

the British Museum
saved everything
illegal or not

was often diverted to explore other interesting matters for their own sake.

This required a prodigious amount of slogging. It was quite a normal day for me to begin in the library at 9 A.M. and end in my own room at midnight or after. I had to sift through a colossal amount of material to fashion the final mosaic of my thesis chapters.

I was helped substantially in the tedious labor because Esther would come along to the library, and as I made note of useful excerpts she would copy them, check them for accuracy and have them available for later use.

Yet for all my labor I discovered during my first year in Edinburgh that the Scottish library lacked some of the records required to trace the myriad activities of the Clapham fraternity. That library, for example, used not to preserve illegal publications—books and papers printed without paying the tax required at the time.

The British Museum even in those days saved everything, illegal or not. I was advised to go to London and see if I could unearth in the British Museum material not preserved elsewhere.

So in June, 1933, Esther and I left Edinburgh for London. We made the trip a holiday, meandering south by bus through all the loveliness of Scotland and England. We went to Gretna Green, Carlisle, the Lake District, on down to Stratford-on-Avon—where in the new Memorial Theatre we saw *The Taming of the Shrew*—and on to Oxford, where we visited the great Bodleian Library. It was a pleasant beginning to what was to be a memorable summer.

Working at the British Museum was in itself a great experience. The University of Edinburgh had given me accreditation as a research student. From then on I had not only the resources of the library but of the librarians. In the British Museum they all seemed to be scholars. They did not only bring books. They took an interest in what the reader was doing. They were always ready to join in a search for relevant material. They never played the numbers game

a sizable block of my program was the time I spent in jail

about books on the desks. I had my own place and I used to have books around me in piles. My summer at the museum library was of crucial help to me in finding material in century-old sources that I could not have unearthed by myself.

My work at the museum pointed me to further sources of material. I got permission to search through the vaults of the British and Foreign Bible Society and delve into long untouched records, reports and documents of the first years of that ancient institution. I pored also over the records of annual meetings of another institution which was a legacy of Clapham piety, the then vigorous Religious Tract Society. I went out to Clapham itself and examined old records and pictures with the Rev. T.C. Dale, the scholarly custodian of the Clapham Antiquarian Society. I went to Hull, and spent some days going through the documents, artifacts and archives of the Wilberforce Museum, that memorial to "the very sun of the Claphamic system," William Wilberforce himself.

I am glad I went there. That building with its unmatched documentation of the institution of slavery was obliterated in the bombing raids of World War II. I had looked through a great deal of material, and made use of some which can never be examined again.

At the end of the summer, a time during which my work on my thesis was lightened and enlivened by delightful exploration of the city of London itself and its environs, we went back to Scotland to spend the final work on the thesis in easy contact with my tutors, Dr. Hugh Watt and Dr. Harry Miller.

By now I was beginning to see how the outlines would be shaped and how they would be filled. There was still a lot of slogging left. By the time I had that dissertation ready for submission—which was not to be till after I had left Scotland—I had written it from beginning to end five times: first by hand, for I was then not quite at ease with a typewriter; then a revised version in my own dreadful typing; then a version revising the revision; then the final draft; and at last the final draft covered with corrections, retyped by a stenographer who could do a job fit for presentation to the University.

While my university work was the centre of all my activities, it was by no means the circumference. In particular, I had one enterprise which took a sizable block of my week's program: it was the time I spent in jail—not sentenced there, employed there.

When I went to Scotland I had in mind the possibility of augmenting my limited finances by getting an assistantship at a city church. Despite my Methodist background, I had acquired, as a minister of the United Church of Canada, the status of an ordained Presbyterian. But before I found any opening as assistant, I ran—as usual, by unexpected chance—into a quite different but exciting prospect: becoming a chaplain in a Scottish jail.

On the outskirts of Edinburgh, Saughton Prison was a new, large and supposedly model prison. It took prisoners whose sentence was not over three years, or if over three years whose age was under eighteen. A prisoner under eighteen sentenced to more than three years was kept at Saughton until he reached maturity—his eighteenth birthday. (One of the most hardened criminals I met was a boy who at age sixteen had murdered a charwoman by bashing in her skull, and then, with the few shillings he got, had gone off to a movie).

In Saughton Prison the Protestant chaplain had by law to be Presbyterian, though he was chaplain to all the Protestants (which in Edinburgh meant nearly all the prisoners). In the good Old Country way, however, the official Chaplain got the appointment—and I suspect most of the emolument—but then hired someone else to do most of the work. As a minister of the United Church, I was eligible.

I was interviewed by the chaplain and was promptly hired. And so, within a few weeks of my landing in Scotland, though I had never in my life been in a jail, I was, to my great surprise, chaplain of a large Scottish penitentiary.

My main duties were to take one service every second Sunday morning and go out two evenings each week and interview the Protestant prisoners who had been admitted since I was there the time before. This I did (with one or two periods of absence) for most of my stay in Edinburgh. In that experience I extended my education into fields not included in my academic calendar.

In Saughton, the Chaplain had a great deal of freedom in dealing with the inmates. When he entered the prison he was given his own ring of keys, which opened all the prison doors except the outer admission and the Death Row. He was supposed to be, as we might put it today, the Ombudsman. Any time any prisoner who felt that he had a grievance had the right to see the chaplain; and the guard under penalty of dismissal was required to inform the chaplain. In my experience, few of the complainers had genuine grievances.

Prison is not a pleasant place; but in those early years at Saughton I found almost nothing of the rough treatment about which we have recently been hearing in Ontario.

When the chaplain had finished his calls on his new customers (I would write my reports at home afterwards) he was free to visit the prisoners he had met before. Curiously, the chaplain was almost always welcomed cordially, especially when he dropped in to see the longer term inmates with whom he had become familiar. The explanation was that the Saughton prisoners were each in a separate cell, and they had lonely hours. They were far more receptive to a visit from a minister than they would have been outside.

Loneliness too, I feel, was what made it so easy for us to get a good choir for the Sunday service. The members of the choir, instead of spending the weekend in their cells alone, could get together Friday night and have a delightful time at choir practice. I had one repeater who was a Roman Catholic but who booked himself in as a Protestant because he was musical and wanted to get in the choir. The guards knew the truth but nobody made a fuss.

In time, I concluded from my interviews that I had never before been in so large a company all totally innocent. In an almost desperate way, as they told their stories, they strove to maintain some element of respectability for themselves and their families. One lady told me with pride that her sister "had the same kind of eye trouble as the Prime Minister."

I met some extraordinary characters among the prisoners. I remember a professional pickpocket from London. He found the London police too closely on his tail, and by an unfortunate inspiration decided to shift his operations to Edinburgh. On his first morning in his new field, with extraordinarily bad luck, he tried at the entrance of a tramway car to relieve a Scottish housewife of her purse. In no time at all his Edinburgh address was Saughton Prison. He told me a great deal about the comparatively opulent life of pickpockets, the way they practised their craft, singly and together, and their tempting success in living by it.

The record of my interviews ran the gamut of crime from petty theft, drunkenness and prostitution, to large scale embezzlement and murder. (Those charged with murder, if convicted, would be

he told me
about the opulent life
of pickpockets

promoted to the maximum security prison, Peterhead.)

The most distasteful of all my duties was visiting the prostitutes, who were usually charged with being drunk and disorderly. These were the days before penicillin and other wonder drugs. We knew that these unfortunate girls were all dosed with venereal disease. They were doomed and they knew it; and I knew it; and they knew that I knew they knew it. I felt like a hypocrite every time I tried to talk to them. I tried at least not to lower such self esteem as they still possessed. By the time I left Edinburgh, I had a number of girls whom I used to see down town and whom I knew well enough to call by name. I remember one cold and chilly day when I asked one of them to come into a teashop and get a hot cup of tea. As we had tea together, the lady of the place seemed to think that something was going on that shouldn't be.

I don't know if I did any good to any of the prisoners. I hope so, but I doubt that I ever did for the doomed girls of the street.

My appointment as assistant chaplain at Saughton destroyed any chance of my getting an assistantship, but not of supply preaching. I still had every second Sunday free. As time went on and I made more contacts, I got quite a number of preaching engagements. During my second year for ordinary services and for special events, I preached in Dunfermline, Galashiels, Bridge of Allen, Hawick, Inverness and a number of other places. I had some interesting experiences and made some good Scottish friends. In one of the Dunfermline churches the minister was Robert Dobbie, whose wife introduced me to that culinary delight, the Scottish trifle. Many years later Robert Dobbie came to be a professor at Emmanuel College, Toronto, and he and Mrs. Dobbie became members of Bloor Street Church.

My contact with the church at Hawick brought consequence of a different nature. The minister had left and the congregation was looking for a successor. I went there first for a Christmas service in 1933. Throughout the following spring I was invited back for several occasions. After one weekend, a committee of the congregation

131

the chief requisite
of a doctoral thesis—
"main strength and stupidity"

waited on me and asked if I would consider accepting an invitation as their minister.

Esther was with me, and they took us up and showed us the manse, a large old house build solidly of stone, but modern compared to the church, part of which went back, if my memory is right, to the 12th century.

We were surprised, but we both looked upon the invitation with some favor. The prospect of a few years in Scotland was not without appeal. But we feared that if we once got settled we might not find it easy to move. So we reluctantly decided that it would be wiser not to accept the invitation.

And then by a turn of events as spectacular as it was unexpected, I got another invitation. I received a cable from Beverly Hills, California, asking me if I would consider an invitation to the Presbyterian Church there; the pastorate to begin as soon as I found it convenient to return. I was astounded. I could attribute the invitation only to those two Sundays of summer preaching at the Pasadena Presbyterian Church.

During my studies in Scotland I had given little thought to what I would do after graduation. I had perhaps taken it for granted that I would be going back to Canada and would probably be minister in whatever congregation would be charitable enough to take me. I had an inkling that perhaps I might go to the West. From the first time I set out on my inaugural ride on Ruby to my unknown destination, I had had a fondness for the prairies. However, I had given no real thought to the matter. I rested in the Biblical reflection that "sufficient unto the day is the evil thereof."

At first the idea of going to the Beverly Hills Church daunted me. I was afraid that I would be overwhelmed. I thought that I would do better to begin in some less demanding place and learn by experience.

But I remembered Dr. Clarence Mackinnon's repeated counsel that the best way to grow is to get in a place where you have to stretch. I replied to the cable by letter. Other letters followed. And finally

I agreed that when I had finished my time at Edinburgh I would return to California, and there both the church and I could make a final decision.

The business of winding up our affairs now began in earnest. By dint of a good deal of plodding toil in the museum during the day and in my room at night I had my thesis in just about its final stage. I had had review discussions with my advisers and done everything except the tedious details of typing and revising. I had almost come to the conclusion that the chief requisite of a doctoral thesis was, in the old Newfoundland phrase, "main strength and stupidity."

Leaving Edinburgh meant a great deal more than winding up an academic project. We had made many friends, particularly among the large group of American students, with some of whom we have kept in contact ever since. On our own bicycles and in the automobiles of generous Scottish friends, and by bus and train, we had seen much of the beauty and splendor of an historic land, from which came much of our own heritage.

One event in particular we counted a rare privilege. In our first year (1933) we were in Edinburgh during the general assembly of the Presbyterian Church. This is the most colourful and impressive ecclesiastical ceremony in the Protestant world. That year the Lord High Commissioner was John Buchan, two years later to become Governor-General of Canada, and later the first Baron Tweedsmuir. The Lord High Commissioner is the personal representative of the King or Queen then reigning. For the period of the Assembly he lives in Holyrood Palace, and gives sumptuous dinners and a Garden Party a la Buckingham Palace. Through the courtesy of friends, Esther and I were invited both to the palace reception and the garden party. We attended many of the Assembly sessions where we saw and heard many celebrities. We found that week an exciting time. I never dreamed that at a future General Assembly I would be present as the Moderator of the United Church of Canada and would address the Assembly.

However much we had seen in England and Scotland, we had failed in another intention: to get some time on the Continent. We determined, therefore, that whatever the pressure, we would at least take a week to see Paris.

So after a whirl of farewells from our fellow students we headed again to London and thence from Dover to Calais. We spent a crowded succession of days, trying to see in a week what we couldn't

133

cover adequately in a year. We touched the high spots. We happened to be in Paris on Palm Sunday and we went to a service at the Madeleine. Among other places we saw Napoleon's tomb and went up the Eiffel Tower. We went out to Versailles and spent a day there. We spent a day at the Louvre. We were one evening at the Opera, and another at the Folies Bergere. It was a forced-feeding of Parisian culture.

From Paris, after a thrilling week, we caught the boat train for Cherbourg and there embarked for New York on the *Berengeria*. The *Berengeria* was then one of the largest ocean liners afloat. But, in Depression style, she was carrying only a fraction of her full complement of passengers. We had plenty of space; but the winds were raw and once reached gale force. The sea was rough, and Esther was down with a cold, not improved with the complication of *mal de mer*. In the circumstances, Easter Sunday came as something less than prolonged jubilation. But the *Berengeria* ploughed on, and in time we did arrive unscarred in New York. There, after going up to Union to visit friends of the year before, we set out again westward across the continent.

Chapter 12

Beverly Hills

*life among the stars
and the rich
of California*

We reached California April 10th, 1934. I learned that the Los Angeles presbytery had made some engagements for me. On April 15, I preached at Santa Monica, the next Sunday in Los Angeles and the next in the Pasadena Presbyterian Church where I had taken that summer assignment two years before. This interlude made it possible for the Beverly Hills congregation to take second thought before committing themselves to an invitation.

On the first Sunday in May I went by invitation to the Beverly Hills Church. After the close of the service, while I waited in the vestry, a congregational meeting voted to invite me as minister. I was told afterward that there was one dissenting vote—a young lady who marched up to the front seat and defiantly stood up when the others sat down. I am not sure whether she was of some fundamentalist persuasion, or whether she was just wiser than her years.

Unknown to the Beverly Hills congregation an ironic side play had marked those final weeks. At that time the Superintendent of Home Missions in Newfoundland was a man named Oliver Jackson—one of the most outstanding clergymen in the history of Newfoundland Methodism. (Shortly after this he was drowned while on a visit to my former charge at Burgeo.) Jackson was anxious that I come back to Newfoundland. When he heard of the possibility of my going to California he set to work to have me invited to a Newfoundland Church. It happened that in Gower Street Church, the foremost congregation in Newfoundland, (incidentally the church where I was accepted as a candidate for the ministry, and where I was later elected as Moderator) the minister was leaving. Jackson sent a telegram to me in Pasadena asking me not to accept a Beverly Hills invitation until I had heard from Gower Street. He soon found that it was a hopeless task to get the Gower Street congregation to invite me. They pointed out that I was too young and inexperienced to go to a church of such importance. Jackson had to send me a second telegram saying that there would be no invitation.

Far away, where I was unknown, I could be passed off as a bright young Canadian; in my own territory I was just a young probationer without the qualification of experience.

I accepted the invitation to the Beverly Hills Presbyterian Church. That was the beginning of one of the most exciting episodes in my life.

In the days before World War II and the coming of the great industrial complexes, many California cities were places of great beauty; but among them all Beverly Hills was the brightest jewel. Only between ten to fifteen years before I went there, it had been laid out and built in an area previously of bean fields. It had been designed with a double set of streets. Those in front of the houses were gracefully curved, each street lined with a particular variety of shade trees; those behind the houses were for the use of garbage and delivery trucks and other such traffic. The master plan of the city left places for only three churches: Roman Catholic, Episcopalian (Anglican) and Presbyterian. They were on the edge of a park on Santa Monica Boulevard, the city's main thoroughfare. All three were so attractively situated that they were frequently used as props in movie scenarios.

Although Beverly Hills was so new, it was already competing with satellite developments on its fringes. One of these was Bel-Air, even then a glamour stop on the tourist tours. Bel-Air took its name from its developer, a man named Alphonso Bell. He was one of the chief elders of our church, and chairman of the committee which had to recommend its new minister.

At the time I went there, Bell had some financial problems. He owned an enormous area of land in the Bel-Air vicinity, but with the Depression the number of people wanting magnificent houses suddenly shrank. He had to pay large taxes with small revenues. I heard it said that he was down to his last six million. He had only one Rolls Royce, though he had a number of Packards. However, after all these years I count Alphonso Bell one of the finest human beings I have ever known. He was more conscious of the responsibilities of wealth than most people, either rich or poor.

among them all
Beverly Hills
was the brightest jewel

Bell's estate crowned the hill on which Bel-Air was built. It had the best location and was one of the most imposing residences in the area. Bell had not only impressively landscaped his grounds; he had gone to Europe and bought a number of marble statues and other carvings to improve the effect. Like the churches, his house served on more than one occasion as a setting for a movie picture.

Just before we left Beverly Hills, the Bell estate was the locale for a then famous movie, "Cardinal Richelieu," with the lead played by the celebrated English actor, George Arliss. Just as the film was to begin, Mrs. Bell invited Esther and me to have tea with Arliss. We were unable to go, but afterwards in Winnipeg we were able to cross the street from our manse and see the movie, filmed in the Bell grounds that we knew so well.

Just below Bell's residence was the estate of George Hormel, then the third largest meat packer in the U.S., after Swift and Armour. Hormel was another influential leader in our Beverly Hills Church and another remarkable man. He was one of the industrial leaders who believed in high wages. He spent time and money trying to get miniumum wage laws through Congress. In one of the worst years of the Depression, he started a daring experiment in wage policy. He put all his blue collar employees on yearly salary. During that year there were repeated weeks when Hormel's plants were closed. But all his workers were paid their salary. The experiment attracted considerable attention; I remember a *Time* magazine article. But alone Hormel could not, with that plan at that time, meet the competition. So the experiment did not survive. There were not too many men in business like George Hormel.

Hormel had an estate that in every aspect except elevation rivalled Bell's. He also had elaborate grounds and he delighted in giving the most marvellous barbecues with extraordinarily fine steaks expertly cooked by his own chef. Esther and I were there on different occasions.

From the beginning Hormel was a warm friend of mine, I might almost say, fan. He gave me my first pulpit gown—and thereby

The gown on which I saved a millionaire $5!
I'm standing in the side door
of the Beverly Hills Presbyterian Church.

---

hangs a tale. When I went to Beverly Hills I did not have a gown so I just preached without one. Hormel asked me if I had a gown, and when I said "No," he said, "Get the best one you can and bring me the bill." So I went to a Los Angeles tailor who specialized in gowns and I bargained with him to get the cheapest rate for the best gown he could make. In the depression slump the price was $100.00; but by hanging on—and certainly not telling him that George Hormel was paying—I got the price down to $95.00.

One night, a few days after I sent the bill to Hormel, his house was robbed. Thieves got into his safe, a small residential one. They cleaned it out. Their take in bills and negotiable paper was $750,000.00. And I had felt so virtuous about bargaining down the tailor, who probably needed the money, and saving Hormel $5.00.

The police never found Hormel's money nor solved the mystery of the theft. But at least I had my gown. It was the best one I ever had. I have it still.

While many of our Beverly Hills congregation were generous in their hospitality, our most regular hostess was from outside the congregation; Miss Mary McCormick, daughter of Cyrus McCormick, inventor of the reaping machine. Miss McCormick had a mansion in Pasadena, but she spent half the year in a "summer home" near Santa Monica on the shore of the Pacific a few miles from Beverly Hills. The scale of the summer home is indicated by the fact that it had a staff of thirty servants.

Miss McCormick, then probably well on in her sixties, was a talented person. She read widely, was interested in literature, art and music, and was herself an accomplished pianist. But she was a schizophrenic and needed care and sensitive supervision. Miss McCormick herself and all her business affairs were managed by a remarkably competent companion and business executive, a Miss Walker, who was the unmistakable boss of the whole establishment. Miss Walker was a former Canadian, as were four of the five Registered Nurses kept on full time staff to look after Miss McCormick's every need.

Shortly after I arrived in Beverly Hills, Miss Walker and Miss McCormick came to our church for Sunday service. The next Sunday they came back and invited us to dinner. That grew into a habit. For the last months we were in Beverly Hills we went without fail after the Sunday morning service to the McCormick estate for midday dinner. In addition, we sometimes went down Saturday afternoon for a swim in the Pacific. The dinner was quite a performance. When we arrived at the door, the butler would be waiting to usher us in, and if we had our new baby, Margery, he would have one of the nurses waiting to look after the baby until we left. Inside the house we first came to the music room. This was where Miss McCormick had her own private orchestra—all of them professionals. On more than one occasion, Esther and I finished our swim, went in to have a cup of tea with our two hostesses, and sat there with a first-class private orchestra playing to the four of us.

For dinner itself, we went to a magnificent dining room with extraordinarily beautiful—almost Newport style—furniture; and nearly as many servants as there were people at the table.

Miss McCormick was an enthusiastic croquet player, and she had in the grounds a beautiful croquet court. But the California sun was often hot. So when necessary, all the players had to do was touch a button. High overhead a canvas awning would roll out over the whole croquet court.

In World War II, the McCormick estate was taken over by military authorities and made into a convalescent hospital for servicemen wounded in the Pacific campaigns. I am glad that so beautiful a place was put to such good use.

My visits there introduced me to a scale of living conspicuously different from that to which I had become accustomed in the parsonages of Newfoundland—or to anything that a minister's salary has since permitted me to emulate.

Because we were in Beverly Hills so short a time, we had no great contact with the celebrities of the movie world, though we were living in the midst of them. Joe E. Brown, a then famous comedian, lived on our street just a few doors from us. His two boys (one later killed in World War II) went to our Sunday school. Fred Astaire's mother used to come regularly to our church. Once when she invited me to tea at the Beverly Hills Hotel, Fred's sister Lady Cavendish was there. But I never met Fred. The mother of a well-known ribald comedian, Jack Oakie, came regularly to church. She told me that she was the widow, the daughter, the granddaughter and the great granddaughter of Methodist ministers. It hadn't rubbed off on Jack. A young woman from Pickfair, the famous residence of Mary Pickford and Douglas Fairbanks (I think a niece of Mary's) used to come to our young people's group—and that connection created a bit of excitement. In the California custom of taking groups of carolers to neighbouring houses at Christmas time, I was leading two or three cars of our teenagers and as previously arranged we went to Pickfair. Mary Pickford came out on that famous balcony to greet the group. But she, or someone, set off the automatic burglar alarm. Before we left the place was swarming with police cars. It added a little spice to the evening.

Will Rogers—though not a member—was one of the earliest supporters of the Beverly Hills Church. I had made an appointment to see him about a campaign for finances just as he was getting ready for his round-the-world trip with Wiley Post. The flurry of preparation made it necessary to postpone our meeting until after his return. Alas! Rogers and Post disappeared somewhere in the Arctic. Our church and the whole world lost something more than money. In due course I conducted in our church a Memorial Service for the man acclaimed as Beverly Hills' "best loved citizen."

Only a few blocks from our house on Camden Drive was a haunt of celebrities, the Brown Derby Restaurant. Above all other water holes, that was then the resort of "everybody who was anybody." We were taken there a couple of times; the place was swarming with the movie elite. The Brown Derby held its pre-eminence for many years. Finally it lost out as it earned the epitaph: "Nobody goes there any more; it's too crowded."

One aspect of my Beverly Hills experience, which supplements the pleasant relations I had with my parishioners, was the warm fraternity I had with an exceptionally fine group of neighbouring ministers in Los Angeles and Pasadena. I was younger than most of them, a newcomer and a Canadian. I doubt that if any youthful American happened to be similarly called to one of the larger Canadian churches he would have found so friendly a reception.

Perhaps it was because I was not as pressed with endless engagements, as I came to be in later years, that in California I developed close and continuing friendships with other clergymen to a degree I have never been able to do since. At the centre of this was a sort of fraternity started by Robert Freeman of Pasadena. That company would meet monthly to give papers, discuss issues or just have a social gathering. I was invited to that company and greatly enjoyed the comradeship.

In short, my time in Beverly Hills was a great experience for me, one which I still remember with pleasure and gratitude. I had warm friends in the congregation. I was living in a natural paradise. I had begun to wonder whether I would be there for the rest of my days. Yet it turned out that in less than two years I was back in Canada and of all places, in Winnipeg. How did that happen?

At the time that I was in Beverly Hills, one of the most celebrated congregations in Canada was Westminster Church in Winnipeg. From its founding in 1893, when Winnipeg was a fledgling city, it

141

had had only four ministers, all of them men of exceptional distinction. The current minister was John Sutherland Bonnell, though we who knew him never called him anything but Sidney, or, more frequently, Sid.

Sid Bonnell was a veteran of World War I, a graduate of Pine Hill a few years before me, and a minister of conspicuous talent as a preacher and as a promoter of causes. He had been in Westminster Church for five years, and by his extremely effective preaching, and his skilful use of international celebrities for special missions, he had built up an enormous popular following. The church used to be packed, and at times the movie theatre across the street was also packed with overflow. In the spring of 1936, at the climax of his remarkable ministry, he was invited to become minister of Fifth Avenue Presbyterian Church, New York.

A few weeks after I heard this news, I was astonished to receive a letter from Westminster Church asking me to come to Winnipeg to take a month's Sunday services during the approaching summer. It was clearly intimated that I was being considered as a successor to Bonnell, and that the holiday preaching would give all a chance to consider the matter. This was completely unexpected. Whatever I had been thinking of, Winnipeg was not within the compass of my thought. (I learned, in time, that attention had been directed to me by Dr. Clarence Mackinnon, who before going to Pine Hill had been a minister of Westminster Church, and who wanted me back in Canada.)

However, though I was not thinking of any immediate move, I still felt that I might some day come back to Canada, and I thought that it was all to the good to keep in touch. So I accepted an invitation that had come as unexpectedly, and that turned out to be as pivotal, as the earlier one which took me to Beverly Hills.

From that time, I began to think a great deal about what I should do with my future years. I was privileged in my position. My situation in Beverly Hills was in many ways ideal, but there were some things that troubled me.

We were living in the Depression. Beverly Hills was an island completely surrounded by Los Angeles, a city which had 500,000 people on relief. Los Angeles had some of the most squalid poverty in all California; Beverly Hills had no relief problem of its own and therefore had low taxes, while its citizens were the second wealthiest group in the United States.

This was shortly after the Lindbergh kidnapping and many wealthy people lived in almost paranoic fear. We had children coming to our Sunday school not only with chauffeurs but with armed guards. Alfonso Bell himself had three Great Danes which he let loose in his grounds at night.

I was not of that company. I lived among them because I was a minister provided with a manse. I was so happily situated that the difference did not trouble me. But when our first child, our daughter Margery, was born, I began to wonder about bringing up a family where our children would not at all be in the same economic class as their comrades.

I came to the conclusion that, fortunate as I was at the moment, Beverly Hills was perhaps not the place for me to raise a family.

A further stimulus to my thinking may well have been the challenge of going at an early age—I was thirty-two—to a church which many observers of the time might consider the most dynamic congregation in the United Church of Canada. I wondered if I could follow Bonnell and somehow do better than anything as yet accomplished.

I soon learned that I was not suited to do what Bonnell had done, but at least I had wisdom enough not to try. When my ministry was over, I think that the majority of the Westminster congregation would say that both Bonnell and I had served the congregation well. But neither one of us did what the other did.

Finally the scale may have been tipped in favor of Winnipeg because I was in perhaps the most idealistic stage of my life. I felt a challenge to assure myself that I had the inner stamina to leave something that was pleasant and secure and take something that was risky and uncertain.

I preached for my four Sundays in Winnipeg. And before I left to return, a congregational meeting of Westminster Church voted to invite me to be their minister. I gave no commitment except that I would take time to consider. For the next two weeks, I was pulled in two directions. Indeed, I composed with great care two telegrams—one accepting the invitation and one rejecting it. I went around several days carrying both in my pocket, not wanting to send either. It was not till the last day of the time within which I had promised my reply that I made the choice. I would go to Westminster. A momentous episode in my life was over.

Westminster United Church in Winnipeg
to which I was called from Beverly Hills

Chapter 13:

Winnipeg

*cold winters
and warm hearts*

The move from Beverly Hills to Winnipeg was the crossing of a great divide. It determined that I was to spend the rest of my days as a Canadian. For good or ill—perhaps for good *and* ill—it affected the whole range of my life experience.

To begin with, there was the weather. We left Beverly Hills in early October in what was still in that paradise a long drawn out delight of summer weather. We landed in Winnipeg in the midst of an untimely intrusion of winter. A fierce wind was blowing and snow whirled in the air. It was the beginning of the worst winter in Winnipeg's recorded history. When we got off the train, all the clothes we had for Margery were the beautiful things designed for Beverly Hills. We managed to wrap her in some spare garment from someone on the reception committee, and got her to the manse.

That day was an omen. For the next six weeks the weather got steadily worse. Then winter set in.

The manse at that time was a huge house, built in 1912 when large houses were in fashion. It was of three stories, with centre halls, front and back stairs; and, I think, something over forty large storm windows to be put on and taken off each year. It also had a furnace, a vast cavern into which we shovelled a ton of coal a week—and took out the clinkers every morning. (Fortunately in a few years we switched to a greatly superior system of heating peculiar to Winnipeg: piped-in hot water coming from central heating plants, making use of Winnipeg's surplus electricity.)

Though we did not know it when going through that first cold winter, we were facing, within six months, the hottest summer Winnipeg had yet known. For four days in succession, temperatures soared to

110 degrees, and newspapers featured photographs of people frying eggs on the burning sidewalks. Fortunately by then we were on our summer holidays at Minaki. It was the first summer of many that we were to spend in the incomparable Lake of the Woods area.

The weather was a factor we learned to accept. I came to like Winnipeg greatly. Many years later it was only with a great wrench that I was able to move away to Toronto. For years after that I was a Winnipegger at heart.

Curiously, my stay in Winnipeg, (I went at age thirty-two and remained till I was forty-five) was the first time since Blackhead back in Newfoundland that I stayed in one place as long even as four years. I was in Halifax for five university years, but for that period I was somewhere else nearly half the time.

Though Margery was born in California, she came to Winnipeg in infancy. Two boys David and George were born in Winnipeg, and all three began their schooling there. So I had roots in Winnipeg as in no previous place of residence.

One further aspect of my Winnipeg years: They were the first time in my life—save that one return trip to Beverly Hills—that I had an annual vacation with pay. The Westminster congregation gave its minister two months holiday. And for me that was a life preserver. I

Esther, Margery and me.
October 12, 1935,
shortly after our arrival
in Winnipeg.

Our family grows.
David joins Margery, with me,
in front of our
Westminster manse.

not only got time out at the lake—the nearest substitute for salt water—I got time to do extra reading and writing. With the schedule I had through the rest of the year, I desperately needed that summer time of recuperation. My years were marked not from January to January but from vacation to vacation. At the end of January I was "half way to the lake." Most of whatever resilience kept me through the winter was the therapeutic residue from my summer place on Menzie's Island in the Lake of the Woods.

The paramount change that Winnipeg brought to my pattern of daily life came from my being minister of Westminster Church. Westminster was a large, extremely well organized—perhaps over-organized—congregation with a great deal of prestige in the city and the province. Its minister was not only meshed in the wheels of its own varied activities, he was involved in an endless procession of outside events: addresses to clubs and lodges, membership in boards and societies, and the annual crop of appeals to go somewhere for anniversary services. I made it a rule to take one anniversary each fall, and perhaps one extra in the spring. The anniversaries, in fact, were a sort of holiday from the weekly grind of preparing two sermons.

Those two sermons Sunday morning and evening week in and

*Father and Mother, taken some time in the late 1930's
after Father received his doctoral hood.*

147 D·D· HONORIS CAUSA
PINE HILL
EmH

*Old skills come in handy. At our Lake of the Woods cottage,
while rebuilding a wharf 80 feet long and 8 feet wide,
I squared timbers with a broad-axe.*

week out were a dreadful incubus. I put an enormous amount of time in their preparation, habitually working in my office late in the evenings.

Almost without exception I dictated them both and had the text in typescript by Saturday. But I had to give up my previous practice of speaking without notes. In the steady grind of busy days I was simply unable to prepare two sermons and deliver them relying solely on the fleshly tablets of memory. I came to depend on notes and I have no doubt that I lost something of a fluency I once had. I have been told, and it may be right, that I was not as good a speaker in my later years as I was earlier.

The Westminster Church building was built like an ancient cathedral, with walls of solid stone. It was and is outwardly a structure of magnificence. The interior was poorly designed and made worse when it was later reconstructed and "modernized." Its seating capacity, including the gallery at the back, was upwards of 1100, and at times that was inadequate for the congregation. On Easter Sundays we would always need to have two morning services.

The peaks of Sunday attendance were the communion services, which, in the Scottish fashion, Westminster celebrated four times a year, following a solemn preparatory service on Friday night. Membes brought their communion cards to present on admittance. (If the card was left at home, another would be supplied.) Visitors also were given cards. Then, on entrance to the sanctuary, each worshipper would deposit the card in the appropriate slot in a cabinet near the door. This complex but well administered system had two results: 1) The session could monitor the attendance at communion of every individual member, and note those negligent in this duty (then considered highly important). 2) The head usher, when the congregation was settled, could hand the minister a slip telling him the localities from which visitors had come. I did not mention names but merely places and they were often of singular diversity. I would give a special word of welcome to our visitors from Brandon, Manitoba; Brisbane, Australia; Glasgow, Scotland; and so on. Visitors who did not know the system were frequently astonished as to how the minister knew.

The Westminster congregation had been well indoctrinated in the Scottish concept of the importance of communion. If we had a congregation of less than a thousand, unless it were desperately bad weather, we would be disappointed. At times we had more than the pews could take, even after we had sent the children out for their own service. To preach to such a packed audience of committed church folk was itself an inspiration.

My years in Winnipeg were marked with the gloom of two dark shadows: first the Depression and Drought, then the second World War.

In our early years, children from some of the dried-out areas of the prairie could come to Winnipeg and for the first time in their lives see green grass. The nadir of the drought period was probably 1937, the year when the prairies had "nothing of everything." During that period our Thanksgiving services in the fall would be times for bringing to the church massive amounts of fruits, vegetables and other foods to ship as relief for farming areas in desperate need farther west.

Yet in time of drought, as in time of war, day follows day and much of life does go on. It would take a volume in itself to tell the story of Westminster Church through these years; of the Actimist Club, the Young Men's Club; the Young Women's Club, the missionary society, the war activities, the coming of casualties, and above all of the many dedicated individuals who by the quiet splendor of their lives touched other lives for good. I cannot even list their names; but they will be given their proper place in the Heraldry of Heaven.

I shall mention only two congregational events of all that passing time: two anniversaries of Westminster Church.

The first in 1937 was a silver anniversary, the 25th anniversary of the opening of the new church building, the magnificent two-towered structure which is still Westminster Church, Winnipeg. One of the many projects of that celebration was a special service in which two former Westminster pastors, Dr. Clarence Mackinnon in Halifax and Dr. David Christie in Victoria, would preach on a Sunday evening across four thousand miles to their old congregation in Winnipeg.

I had read that a huge industrial concern in the United States had worked out a program that for the time represented a new triumph for the telephone. Officials from across the continent spoke by an amplified telephone hook-up to a meeting at the Head Office. I decided that I would make use of the idea.

In 1937, Dr. Mackinnon and Dr. Christie were both still living but were in poor health and unable to come to Winnipeg. So I rented in advance, for twenty minutes, the entire telephone system in Canada from Atlantic to Pacific. In Westminster Church we had the telephone receiver amplified by four loudspeakers, each six feet long. (The instruments in those days were crude compared to those now commonplace.)

Dr. Christie and Dr. Mackinnon, sitting by their respective oceans, could not see us in Winnipeg and could not hear us. All each knew was that, without cue, each must begin preaching a sermon at an exact moment, and end at an exact moment.

The service was planned for Sunday evening, and the church was crowded beyond capacity. I conducted a service arranged for the oc-

150

casion, and at the agreed moment, instead of beginning myself to preach, I introduced Dr. Mackinnon from Halifax. I was in some trepidation. By dismally bad luck we had poor weather conditions across the whole 4000 miles of our rented telephone lines. But I made the introduction and I paused. In seconds a voice familiar to many in the congregation came through those loud speakers, and Dr. Mackinnon in Halifax preached to us in Winnipeg.

When he was finished I thanked him and introduced Dr. Christie. Again, in a matter of seconds, the voice of Dr. Christie came through from Victoria, B.C.

For Westminster Church it was a momentous occasion. It proved to be the last time either Dr. Christie or Dr. Mackinnon would speak in Winnipeg. Both of them died shortly afterward.

If my memory is right, I paid $85 for that twenty minutes. It took great preparation, for such a service had never been conducted in Canada before; I doubt if one has since.

The 1937 Silver Jubilee was so successful that six years later I planned and carried out a Golden Jubilee! This feat was not as impossible as it seems. The Silver celebration was the anniversary of the new church building; the Golden was the anniversary of the congregation.

In 1943, we were deep in World War II. Many of our young men

We never did get Esther's parents to Newfoundland,
but in 1936 both sets of our parents met in Winnipeg:
The Howses are on the left, the Blacks on the right.

were gone; and everything that happened was set against the sombre background of a life and death struggle. We brought Dr. Bonnell and his family from New York and had him as the main speaker of the occasion. That was not as dramatic as having Christie and Mackinnon preach by telephone, but we did one other thing which may be of interest some years ahead.

At that time, we had no tape recorders. The only instrument for reproducing sound was the standard Gramophone record. So I got the necessary equipment to cut a record conveying the greetings of Westminster Church on its 50th anniversary to those who would be celebrating on its 100th anniversary.

Dr. Bonnell and I both made addresses of greeting, as did a number of others including Isaac Pitblado, son of the founding minister. That record, I presume, will be heard by Westminster members when the congregation celebrates its centenary in 1993—not so far in the distance. So I shall be conveying a welcome to the then Westminster members when the congregation rounds out its century—and I have long since been dead.

Anniversary celebrations, whatever their immediate effect in renewal of personal friendships and revival of congregational loyalty, were nevertheless only times of passing interest. The regular work of the church went on and the increasing demands of daily life gradually crowded my days more and more.

Early in my Winnipeg ministry I began the practice of using the evening service as a time for dealing with current issues of social and ethical concern. In the fall of 1937, on two successive Sunday evenings, I preached sermons on the extraordinary threat to democracy in two laws the passage of which had shocked Canadians: The "Padlock Law" of Quebec and the "Accurate News Act" of Alberta. Both laws would control the press in every word it could print. The Quebec law would give the premier power to confiscate any book which, in the premier's opinion was, "tending to propagate Communism"—plato's *Republic* as well as Marx's *Das Capital*.

Both Winnipeg newspapers gave editorial commendation to my presentation of the issue, and printed almost the entire text in their news column.

From this time on I seemed to be regarded as a representative of the liberal point of view on everything, religious or secular. Indeed, even before this I had been approached by some striking fur workers to take up their cause. I had just begun when the strike collapsed.

152

I preached
on the extraordinary
threat to democracy

On another occasion I was asked by the Hutterites to plead their cause before a legislative committee. This I did and helped, I hope, in staving off legislation that would have been a disgrace to the province.

Once I even made an appeal to have certain Communists released from jail. It was after Russia had entered the war. Suddenly a number of Communists, who were in jail for opposing our war effort, began pleading for permission to go to Russia to fight against their erstwhile comrades the Nazis. My position was that any Communist who wanted to go to Russia should be given every possible assistance to get there! At a "Citizens' Rally" in the Walker Theatre, sponsored by Communists, I was one of four speakers (two of them Communists) who advocated removal of the war-time ban on the Communist party, release of Communists in jail, and permission, for all who would, to go to Russia and fight the Nazis. Mr. Tonkin, Counsellor of the Russian Legation, wrote me that it was "an excellent speech." Dr. John Dafoe of the Winnipeg Free Press said that it was an "argument well and honestly done."

Only the conditions of a world war could have put me on the platform at a Communist rally.

The ban on the Communist party—an ill-advised move which the Canadian government soon had sense enough to repeal—was not the only war-time policy to which I publicly objected. When the War Measures Act was proclaimed, I joined with some members of the Winnipeg Civil Liberties Association to draft an analysis pointing out some of the inherent dangers of that heavy-handed legislation. I also wrote to a number of other Canadians in other parts of Canada asking them to join in our protest.

In addition, on different occasions, in sermons and in conversation, I objected to the way the Japanese of British Columbia were being treated. Now I regret that I did not pursue that issue more vigorously.

One cause to which I was ardently committed was the struggle to shift the Canadian government to a more human policy on refugees—particularly the Jewish refugees fleeing from the monstrous cruelty of the Nazis. It is difficult now to understand the mental climate of the Depression years. Opposition to refugees was not limited to Jewish refugees. Opposition was to immigrants of any kind who might come to Canada and take jobs. The opposition was almost universal but it was centred in two focal points: the labour unions and the province of Quebec. In Quebec the most conspicuous fascist rabble-rouser in North America, Adrian Arcand, with his following of thugs in blackshirts, fanned the flames of nationalism and anti-semitism.

To advocate the admission of immigrants, particularly of refugees who, so it was argued, might be spies for Hitler, was to enter the lists in an extremely unpopular cause.

In April, 1939, when the pressure on fugitives from Hitler was desperate, and when the Canadian government was unyielding in its hostility to refugees, I preached two evening sermons (the first one broadcast) in a plea for admittance to Canada of the victims of Hitler's tyranny. Both newspapers gave the appeal extensive coverage and editorial commendation. I got a deluge of letters, some of them bitterly hostile, and in response I had the sermons printed in pamphlet form, available to those who asked. We distributed several thousand, far and wide across Canada. Recently Gerald Dirks, author of *Canada's Refugee Policy* told me that in his research for that book, he found, so long afterwards, copies of that sermon in the files of a Senator and of a Leader of the Opposition.

The desperate years of the war brought—alas, too late—a change in the mindset of many Canadians. An increasing number of influential citizens became convinced that Canada's refugee policy had been shameful, and that even in time of war something might be done to bring some of the homeless ones safely to Canada.

Carine Wilson, a pioneer lady Senator, organized a Canadian National Committee on Refugees. Such a committee, she thought, could mobilize the growing Canadian sentiment to do something about the refugee situation. A young woman, Constance Hayward, set out to organize branches in the larger Canadian cities. She wrote to me before she arrived in Winnipeg, and a few of us set up a meeting of influential citizens who in turn recruited an impressive number of leaders in Winnipeg life. The full committee soon included the Premier, the Mayor, two Archbishops and a roster of

154

other celebrities. Sidney Smith, President of the University of Manitoba, was elected Honorary Chairman; I became Active Chairman. There was only one reason that I, a clergyman not yet out of his thirties, was elected to such a position by such a company. It was that for several years I had been persistently advocating the policies which the Canadian National Committee on Refugees was now beginning to adopt.

Unfortunately, the Canadian National Committee on Refugees became geared for action too late. The first company of Refugees which the Winnipeg Branch, through the tediously slow process of wartime bureaucracy, brought to their city, was also the last. After that the Canadian government passed the problem of refugees to the new United Nations Relief and Rehabilitation Association.

That one company which we did manage to bring over from Spain (where they had fled, after suffering bitter hardships, from countries as far away as Hungary and Bulgaria) were an interesting group. Altogether there were six families, 19 individuals. One family, the Torals, was Christian, the others Jewish. They included two doctors

During the war, we gained a fifth member of the family, George, (just behind Margery) and two temporary guests, John and Marjorie Newton from England, in the centre front.

On Lake of the Woods, Margery soon learned to take charge of running our boat.

and an opera singer. When a small group, consisting of members of the Jewish Volunteer Bureau, Dr. Ernest Hunter and I met them at the railway station, the last stop on their flight for freedom, it was an emotional moment. We had no difficulty in providing them with suitable lodging, clothes and food. They soon proved to be no burden but an asset to Canada.

In earlier days a small group of us in Winnipeg had joined with other Canadians in two attempts to bring refugee children to Canada. We found that a substantial number of Canadians would be willing to provide foster homes for the considerable number of waifs and orphans picked up and brought to England in the wake of the Nazi conquest of Europe.

But it is a significant commentary of the time that there was no official sympathy for bringing any orphans to Canada, under any scheme. I had a letter from Department of Health and Welfare of the Manitoba government, rejecting the idea by a transparent device. They stated that orphans could be admitted to Canada only when they had "a certificate of death of both parents." The problem was that the children picked up in the flight from the Nazis had no papers and no way of getting any. So the proposal was impaled on that Catch 22.

A little later, the bombing of Britain brought a different response. A large contingent of British children, intended to be the forerunner of many others, was put on a steamer and shipped across the Atlantic. Of these, about 250 came to Manitoba, of whom 200 were taken to Winnipeg.

That plan did not survive. Two important considerations stopped it at the start. First there was the terrible danger of one of these ships crowded with children being torpedoed. Second, more careful thought suggested that to pick up children from London, or anywhere else, and scatter them throughout Canada, only to send them back again after the war to the homes they had left, might cause more stress than sticking it out with their families. So the first contingent was the last.

As one of the chief Winnipeg promoters of this scheme, I felt it incumbent upon me and our family to do our share. So we took two of these children, a brother and sister, John and Marjorie Newton. Both were with us for about a year, and then some friends who had girls in the family but no boys shared the task by taking John.

Marjorie stayed with us till the end of the war. We had some

156

I met them at the station
the last stop
on their flight for freedom

minor problems. For example, Marjorie had a tubercular ulcer on her chest. But the doctors in Winnipeg were able to clear that up. Both found some difficulty of adjustment at the beginning, but not as much as they did on their return. However, they pulled through.

Another episode of Canadian wartime, little known but poignant, was the plight of the student internees. These were boys, anti-Nazis who before the war had fled Germany, and who until May, 1940, had been living in sanctuary in England, known and classified as friendly aliens. In the immediate peril of invasion, the British government interned all such aliens, and sent about 2400 of them to be interned in Canada. Later, the British government called back about 900 of military age for various forms of national service. But, incredibly, the Canadian government for over a year left the younger boys, most of whom had been in school in England, still interned, and with practically no one in Canada knowing anything about it.

Then the Canadian government offered to release the boys of school and university age, if Canadian sponsors would undertake their maintenance.

When I learned of the matter, in the fall of 1941, protests had already been made in Eastern Canada but nothing had appeared in the media. (Media was a word not yet coined). So I preached a sermon on the story and wrote letters to both Winnipeg newspapers, which supported me with editorial comment. In a few days we had offers from people willing to be foster parents. In the end, we had quite a few of the boys settled in Manitoba.

If some wartime efforts were pathways to frustration, one which began in the basement of Westminster Church was different. It was a small beginning which led to an enormous enterprise. In the early days of the war it was impossible to ship used clothing from Canada to Britain. Even the Red Cross, by policy, would not take second hand clothing as wartime relief. The theory was that Britain so desperately needed such items as food and war materials that space for clothing could not be given on trans-Atlantic ships.

157

But, when the heavy bombing of Britain began, some of our church women, headed by Mrs. Donald McIntyre—one of the most remarkable individuals I have known—saw clearly that clothing would be one of that beleaguered country's vital necessities. I began to explore the possibility of getting around the ban on used clothing, and to find a way of shipping clothing, especially children's clothing, to the people whose homes were being destroyed.

I wrote both to Lady Tweedsmuir, the wife of John Buchan who had just finished his stint as Governor-General of Canada, and to Mrs. Vincent Massey, the wife of our High Commissioner to Britain, and asked for their counsel. They both warmly approved the idea, but neither knew any way to get a permit to ship used clothes to Britain. Lady Tweedsmuir wrote of the "wonderfully generous offer" and said "Clothes are one of our greatest needs ... Bombed-out people often have ... only the clothes they stand up in."

Finally, after more letters and telegrams, Mrs. Massey suggested

Winnipeg women load parcels to send to war-devastated Europe.
In 1948, when I visited Hamburg, I saw some of these parcels
in a warehouse, awaiting distribution.

that we try shipping parcels personally to her at Canada House.

Mrs. McIntyre went to work. Our ladies parcelled up their accumulated clothes. It was a parcel all right—a ton and a half of clean, good clothing.

We shipped the parcels in February, 1941. They disappeared, and we heard nothing more about them till June. But Mrs. Massey's strategy worked. Her name and her husband's office took the consignment through.

Our shipment arrived a day after one of the heaviest bombings London had yet had. It was a godsend. And when the story got back to Winnipeg, it received instant publicity. It was apparent that here was a program with possibilities. Mrs. Gordon Konantz, an influential Winnipeg citizen (later an M.P.) came to see me and asked about operating this on a larger scale. I was delighted. This was exactly what we wanted.

From there on the movement changed from being a project of the Westminster women, and soon became Manitoba's "Bundles for Britain." The ban on shipping used clothing was lifted. During the war Manitoba sent incredible amounts of clothing, which must have been of immense help to uncounted thousands of bombed-out families.

But the impulse that shattered the inertia and put the whole scheme in motion—aided by the timely arrival of that first bundle of Canadian clothes—came from the mind of one intelligent women and the hands of many helpers in the basement of Westminster Church.

Fortunately for Canadians, wartime obligations, though urgent and intrusive, did not command the whole of life. To an astonishing degree, the normal round of common days kept its accustomed way. Like many others who lived through these days I did what I could to help the war effort, but still nurtured other interests.

One concern which had been kindled during my Beverly Hills ministry was the promotion of better relationships between Christians and Jews. When I began my ministry and for years following, the tremendous anti-semitism generated by the Hitler movement in Europe had considerable overflow in North America. The joint action of Christian and Jew, now so commonplace, was almost completely unknown, and the need for it not widely perceived.

During my Beverly Hills days I went to a seminar conducted by a clergyman, Russel Clinchy, who was starting in the United States what was a new movement—by no means widely popular at the time—to promote better relations between Christians and Jews. I became quite interested in this idea, and soon joined at U.C.L.A., what may well have been the first group formed in that part of the country, in which Protestant and Roman Catholic clergymen met with rabbis to explore the possibilities of a more cordial interfaith climate. Ironically, at that time it was as remarkable for Roman Catholic and Protestant clergymen to meet with one another as it was for them to meet with rabbis.

After my return to Canada, the outbreak of World War II and the sense that all free peoples were in common peril gave a new impetus for bridging old divisions and risking new adventures in inter-faith harmony. In November 1940, under the auspices of the B'nai Brith, I joined with Roman Catholic Bishop Frank R. Wood, and Rabbi Solomon Frank, in a public meeting in the Royal Alexandra Hotel to declare an essential unity underneath our divisions. A couple of years later (by which time we had become good friends), I invited Rabbi Frank to preach at the morning service in Westminster Church.

In Canada, rabbis had previously shared in the more open evening services; but this, I believe, was the first time a rabbi had been invited to preach the sermon in a Christian church at the regular Sunday morning service of worship.

After the war ended, Christmas in the Westminster Manse.

At about the same time I was one of several speakers at a mass meeting of about 4000 people in the Winnipeg auditorium to protest the Nazi persecution of the Jews. My address was entitled, "I speak for the Jew." It was reprinted in the periodical "Fellowship" published by the Canadian Conference of Christians and Jews, and quoted widely in other places. More recently Rabbi Reuben Slonin has quoted favourably from it in his book *Family Quarrel*.

I also was actively engaged in the founding of the Winnipeg branch of the Conference of Christians and Jews. In Canada, the Conference had been promoted and established under the guidance of the United Church clergyman, Claris Edwin Silcox. In Toronto, Silcox and Rabbi Morris Eisendrath were the dynamic leaders of the movement.

Closely associated with these two men was Dr. Ernie Hunter, another United Church clergyman, who moved to Winnipeg and there became my neighbour and friend. He told me about the venture in Toronto and he and I decided to augment the movement by a branch in Winnipeg. We invited Silcox to Winnipeg and arranged a dinner with a substantial number who warmly supported our proposal and set up a committee to proceed with the details of organization. When the nominating committee reported to a later meeting Dr. Hunter, who was still with Rabbi Eisendrath co-chairman of the national movement, was *ex officio* on the Sub-executive; Sidney Smith, President of the University of Manitoba, was chairman; and I was secretary-treasurer. So, with Ernie Hunter as the chief instigator and counsellor, we set up in Winnipeg an organization which continues its valuable service to this day.

One detail is illuminating. The name in those early days was "The Canadian *Conference* of Christians and Jews." The word is now not "Conference" but "Council." Practically all the money which then supported the movement came from a few friends of Silcox's who were Jewish. At the time of the Partition of Palestine, Silcox wrote articles critical of the scheme of partition, saying in effect that it was likely to prove a running sore for future years. This accurate but unpopular prophecy lost him the sympathy of his friends. In a matter of weeks the sources of his support dwindled to a trickle. The office from which he worked was closed, and the periodical he was editing folded.

Then the same men who had supported Silcox, putting out money for the same cause, invited an American clergyman, the Rev.

Richard Jones, to come to Toronto and pick up the movement not as the *Conference* but as the *Council* of Christians and Jews. Silcox felt wronged in the matter; but he held his peace. Today almost no one knows anything about the matter. Few indeed are aware that the name was ever changed.

Dick Jones in the following years did a remarkably good job, and made the Council of Christians and Jews an effective institution of Canadian life. As for our Winnipeg group, we just merged with the new organization.

It is hard now to comprehend what an unusual event it was when that notable group of Winnipeg citizens gathered for that first meeting to promote good will between Gentile and Jew.

An early Winnipeg photo of me.
Used for publicity when I went to preach at anniversaries, etc.

Chapter 14:

Wider Worlds

*the Christian world
and the joy of service*

The varied interests with which the passing years enlarged my life in no way destroyed some which I had had from the beginning—notably the cultivation of unity within the Christian Church itself. I was proud to belong to the United Church of Canada. I had been accepted for the ministry in the Methodist Church. I had been ordained in the United Church. I was still a Methodist; but I was also a Presbyterian and a Congregationalist, and an inheritor of the rich legacy of their traditions. And in my years at Winnipeg, I had watched with intense pleasure the preliminary moves in a venture of another kind—the formation of a World Council of Churches to be established as soon as possible after the end of World War II. When, after years of preparation, hampered by wartime restrictions, the stage was set for the founding Assembly of that Council in Amsterdam in September 1948, I felt that the Christian Church was in the bright dawn of a new and better day.

For years I had kept the Westminster congregation informed about the development of this new movement, but I still was taken completely by surprise when after church service one Sunday morning the Clerk of Session presented me with a cheque to pay the expenses to send Esther and me to Amsterdam for the founding session of that long awaited World Council.

For me this was an enormous thrill. It opened a prospect I had not thought possible. It meant that I could see and hear in person the outstanding leaders of most of the Protestant and many of the Orthodox churches of the world. Names would become faces and persons; and a new venture of Christian faith would be, not a report to

*dumped in their midst
on the verge
of starvation*

be read, but a memory to be cherished.

It added something that the United Church nominated me as an alternate delegate, and the Anglicans, one person short of their possible complement, made Mrs. Howse an Anglican alternate. Perhaps the spirit of the Council was already at work.

Pleased as I was about the chance to go to Amsterdam, I had no knowledge that this was the first step into another unexpected and thrilling experience. To tell that story, I must go back again to some women in Winnipeg.

With the end of the war in Europe, the extraordinary epic of "Bundles for Britain" had come to a close. But a new and even vaster dimension of need had emerged in the war-devastated continent. So church women throughout Canada organized a new association: Canadian Church Relief Abroad (CCRA).

In Winnipeg, the local branch was organized by many of the same women (headed by Mrs. Donald McIntyre and Mrs. Konantz) who had worked in the "Bundles" campaign. In a matter of months the Winnipeg CCRA had shipped to Europe, mostly to Germany, over 45,000 pounds of clothes, including 6000 pounds of shoes. A featured article in the Winnipeg *Tribune* at the time reported that "the local branch was organized by Dr. E. M. Howse of Westminster Church." But I did little more than ask the women to get going again.

The German civilians who survived the war, their misery aggravated by the influx from Eastern Europe of eleven million "expelles" dumped in their midst by the Russians, were on the verge of mass starvation. Dr. Eugene Gerstenmaier, a Lutheran clergyman, who had spent much of the war years as a fugitive in Germany, and who was the sole survivor of a group of twelve designated by the Nazis to die, came to Canada to acquaint church leaders there with the enormity of the need. In Winnipeg, because of the contact I had had with relief work, he invited me to come to Germany and there let *Hilfswerk,* a German relief organization, show me the dimensions of the problems. *Hilfswerk* had no funds for travel, but it would look after me in Germany.

I might perhaps have been inhibited by having to assume travel costs by myself; but my pre-paid trip to Amsterdam had solved the problem. I agreed to go to Germany immediately after the meeting of the World Council.

The proposed trip to Germany opened to me a second pleasing possibility. A Westminster post-war project, more personal than CCRA, had been our assistance to the family of one of the most distinguished German opponents of Hitler.

When World War II ended and individuals who had dared to oppose Hitler within Germany were released from prison, it became clear that some of them had suffered terribly, had been ruined financially, and desperately needed a helping hand. In the United States a Lutheran organization set up a program for getting sponsors to bring to such people personal sympathy and assistance.

I read about this enterprise and wrote to the promoter offering to look after one family. I had no worry about cost; I knew that I would have support from any number of people in the Westminster congregation.

I was given the name of Goerdeler. Karl Goerdeler had been the burgomeister of Leipzig, and came of wealthy and distinguished lineage. He was devoutly religious and while always bitterly opposed to Hitler, was against assassination. However, as the depth of Nazi evil became clear, Goerdeler changed his mind. He was one of those in the plot to kill Hitler by a bomb in a briefcase. When the plot failed both Karl and his brother were caught, tortured and hanged. All the members of both families were sent to prison. The grandchildren were scattered and given different names. It was not until sometime after the war was over that all were found and reunited with their families.

The member of the family with whom I corresponded was Maryann, the oldest daughter of Karl. Her married name was Meyer-Kramer. Her husband was an army doctor. He too had been slated for execution, but was saved by the timing of the allied invasion. All the survivors were in poor health because of deprivation in prison. I wrote to Maryann Meyer-Kramer. Then we began sending parcels to her and through her to her family and others in need. We ordered CARE parcels in a steady stream. We (that is to say the Westminster women) sent our own parcels of food, of clothes, and

Downtown Hamburg in 1948.
I took this picture three years after the end of the war.

of shoes, especially children's shoes. Doctors supplied us with precious parcels of medicines—especially vitamins which Dr. Meyer-Kramer could not get in Germany, and which his patients could not afford.

We were operating almost a personal relief movement of our own. And, at the same time, through the exchange of letters, we were learning of the desperate struggle of life amid the ruins of war. Rations were incredibly low. Fat, I recall, was a pound per person per month. But sometimes no fat was there. Curiously the only rations available in quantity were potatoes and sugar.

I recall being moved by one of the early letters from Maryann telling how, in her first Christmas out of jail, she found somewhere a short piece of candle, and in the cold little room in which she was living she used to light it for five minutes each day to express her thanksgiving.

But, despite the correspondence, I could not help feeling that I was talking to someone from another world. Letters between persons who have never met are a feeble substitute for personal conversation. As soon as I knew that I was going to Germany I knew also that I had another mission. I must visit the Goerdelers.

Everything seemed to be fitting in nicely. I would have my summer holidays. I would have the great experience of being at Amsterdam (plus two ocean voyages). I would have my time visiting post-war Germany. I would come back to another year at Westminster Church brimming over with sermons and speeches. The universe was unfolding as it should.

*Even then, some 80,000 people had no home,
except for hollows under the ruins.*

Then, suddenly, all the happy certainty was shattered. One night as I was working late in my study, the telephone rang, and I heard the voice of an oldtime friend, Sidney Smith, who had previously left Winnipeg to become President of the University of Toronto. After the usual pleasantries he told me that he was speaking to me personally because he was on a committee of Bloor Street Church which had to find a successor to their long-time minister, Dr. George Pidgeon. He had permission to let me know that I was going to be invited and would be asked to come by the first of September. As a friend, he said, he wanted me to accept.

My immediate response was to say "Impossible." To leave so soon after the Westminster congregation had honoured me with such a generous gift would, I felt, not be fitting.

But Smith was not to be so easily put off. We had a long conversation. And I agreed that I would at least take time to think it over.

More calls and conversations followed. The official invitation and letters from Bloor Street officials, even one from Dr. Pidgeon himself, kept the matter on the boil.

One by one, I talked over the matter with my Westminster friends. They were all extremely courteous. All insisted that the coincidence of a gift after thirteen years of service (that was not my first gift) should have nothing to do with my decision.

One aspect of the situation affected me. I was a little scared of the venture. I was happily situated in Westminster Church and was confident that I might have stayed there indefinitely. But at Bloor Street I felt that because of inescapable factors in the city's development, I

167

might be, like many other midtown churches in many other cities, facing a long and uncomfortable decline.

I had in fact somewhat of the same feeling on going to Bloor Street that I had earlier about going to Westminster. And I made the same response. I decided that no one would do much by backing away from what he was afraid of. So I agreed to come to Toronto and talk the matter over with the Bloor Street officials.

After several conversations I agreed to make the move, only stipulating that I should arrive not in September but November. That change would let me bring such reports as I had of the Amsterdam conference to the people who had sent me there.

Once again my life was changed by an invitation that came as a complete surprise.

In August, 1948, Esther and I went to Montreal and embarked on the magnificent ocean liner *Empress of Canada* for our voyage to Europe and our visit to Amsterdam.

Amsterdam had not been physically obliterated by the heavy bombing that had battered London. But it had suffered more from a Nazi occupation that, particularly in the later years, had become an unrestrained orgy of terror, which every day diminished the population by the lingering death of hunger, or the savage violence of bullets and bombs. Of the 80,000 Jews in the city at the beginning, only 6000 survived, and many of these only because of heroic assistance of neighbours and friends. But everybody suffered. The rations for civilians, before the Germans fled, were sufficient only to bring death slowly. In the last terrible months it was a daily chore to pick up from the streets the corpses of those who had collapsed from starvation.

Then it happened, in the impersonal strategy of war, that Canadians swarmed into Amsterdam as the army of liberation. Both privates and officers broke all army rules in sharing their food and scrounging more for the half-starved survivors. When we were there, three years later, it was almost embarrassing to be identified as a Canadian; the thanks of the Amsterdam citizens still poured out so warmly.

As soon as they were freed, the people of Amsterdam, with characteristic industry and intelligence, set to work to repair the ravages of war. They achieved prodigies of restoration; but in 1948 all their accomplishments were gathered together and crowned in two great celebrations; the founding of the World Council of

the light shone out
of the darkness—
the people cheered and cried

Churches; and, immediately afterwards, the investiture of their new Queen, Juliana. The people of Amsterdam saw these two events as a national symbol of their emancipation from the squalor of war.

The historical cathedral, the Nieuwe Kerk (New Church—it was only 450 years old), where the Council and the investiture were to come, was reconditioned throughout and restored to a splendor it had not known for centuries. Outside, it seemed that every Dutchman in the city who could find a square inch of earth had planted flowers. Parks and public squares were beds of orange bloom: marigolds, dwarf dahlias and gorgeous gladiolas. Those who had no flowers hung bunting, red, white and blue, from their windows. The city was a melody of colour.

One particular event touched the hearts not only of the people of Amsterdam but of all Holland. During the war, Amsterdam had become a city of dreadful nights. The Germans had destroyed the electrical systems which had lighted streets and canals.

In the immediate post-war years, the city had been unable to afford reconstruction. But in time, the Dutch engineers got to work. They had a goal—the investiture—and they met it magnificently. They installed new systems of external lighting. They outlined the canals, the bridges, the arches and many of the significant buildings. And then they announced the grand relighting—one night when, at one moment, all the lights would come on at once.

Five hundred thousand people from Amsterdam and outside crowded the streets for that great occasion. The city of Amsterdam provided glass-topped barges for all 1450 people coming in some capacity or other for the World Council of Churches and gave them a tour of the lights in the whole canal system. As we passed by, we could see the streets crowded with jubiliant people.

When the moment came and the light shone out in the surrounding darkness, the people cheered and cried, and then in some places broke spontaneously into the great hymns of their faith.

It was a moment of history. It was a symbol saying as no words ever could that the darkness of the war was over, and light had come again.

It was fitting that the World Council of Churches should be formally constituted in Holland. The prodigious labour of organizing the pioneer meeting of such an assembly had been carried out by a Provisional Committee of fourteen ecumenically minded churchmen who also had met first on Netherland's soil. They came together in Utrecht in May 1938. Despite the war, they continued to meet, proving a valuable instrument of inter-church co-operation, and giving new impetus to the drive for unity. Largely through the work of this Committee, the founding Assembly of the World Council opened with delegates from 150 Churches from 40 countries.

Esther and I attended the opening Service on Sunday, August 22, 1948. In memory I can still see the impressive march of delegates up the centre aisle of the shining new interior of that magnificent cathedral, the Nieuwe Kerk.

In the lead were two young men with banners, one tall and strikingly blonde; the other not quite as tall but of massive stature, and black as ebony.

Behind them came the delegates: black and white and yellow and brown. Some of the lay representatives were decked in the dazzling colours of their national dress, and some of the clergy in brilliant ecclesiastical regalia. The customs of half a hundred countries and the vestments of a thousand years passed in parade.

As the procession marched up that aisle they were singing together, each in his native tongue, that familiar Christian hymn; "All People That on Earth Do Dwell."

I was moved with deep emotion as I reflected that since Jesus had walked in Galilee no company of his followers of comparable diversity of nation and race and creed and colour had ever before assembled "with one accord in one place," anywhere, any time, under any auspices.

A singular feature of that opening service in the Nieuwe Kerk was that the World Council of Churches did not actually exist. The formal constitution of the Council came the next day in the Amsterdam Concertgebouw (Concert Hall), a stately building with a seating capacity of 3000. This was the building where the council met for business sessions, and there on Monday morning, August 23, with the Archbishop of Canterbury in the chair, Pastor Marc Boegner of France presented the formal resolution, "that the World Council of

two young men with banners
one tall and blonde
the other black as ebony

Churches be declared to be, and is hereby, constituted.''

The resolution passed without a single dissent and the packed building burst into applause.

The two opening meetings were the inspirational ones. The toils and debates of following days clearly revealed that a desire for unity does not bridge all the chasms which have historically separated the denominations.

Nevertheless, the founding of the World Council was a great achievement. Many skeptics had believed that the movement would never get off the ground, that it would founder at the start on its own inbred hostilities. The doubters were wrong. The World Council marked the beginning of a new stage of Christian history. It wound up with the stirring phrase, ''We intend to stay together.'' It was not an end, but it was an essential beginning.

The close of the World Council was followed in a matter of days by the coronation of Queen Juliana. The Winnipeg Free Press had given me accreditation as a special correspondent to cover both the Council and the coronation, but I felt it more important to get to Germany to survey the refugee camps and to visit Maryann Meyer-Kramer.   *INVESTITURE*

So, while Esther went off on a tour of her own to visit friends in England and Scotland, I set out across the ruins of Hitler's homeland on my rendezvous with the directors of *Hilfswerk*.

I had no idea how dreadful was the aftermath of the Nazi madness. Three years after the war was over, burned out railway trains still lay by the tracks, shattered sections of the walls of burned apartment houses still had filthy drapes or bed-clothes hanging out the holes that had been windows. In down-town Hamburg, looking out in one direction as far as the eye could see, not one building was left standing. The whole area was as barren as the Sahara desert, only instead of sand it was crumbled brick and rubble, with main streets bulldozed so that vehicles could get through. I was told that, beneath the desolation on which I was looking, 80,000 people were now living

171

in basements where they had burrowed out some sort of shelter.

What made the German situation so desperate was the Russian tactic at the end of the war of dumping more than eleven million unwanted people into Germany, where twenty-five million people were already bombed out. These "expelles" as they were called to distinguish them from the former Displaced Persons, came for the most part with nothing but the rags they stood in. The conditions of the camps which were at first their only shelters, and the starvation rations which were their only food, beggared description. These were the people and the camps *Hilfswerk* wanted me to see.

Since then I have seen some dreadful refugee camps in the Middle East, but none more repulsive or degrading that some of the stockades where the expelles were herded. I left Germany in deep despair. I had no idea of the possible regeneration in a Marshall Plan and the resiliency in the human spirit.

One episode only I must mention, an item which if put in a novel would be regarded as stretching the limits of fiction.

While visiting the city of Hamburg I was taken to the dockside where huge terminals that once had handled the traffic of a continent now were in ruins. In a gloomy corner of an only partially destroyed warehouse I was shown a huge pile of bundles that had just arrived as a relief shipment from overseas. At a word from the official who was conducting me, one of the workmen climbed to the top of the pile and tumbled down a bale which landed right in front of me. I looked at the bale, and I could not believe my eyes. A large familiar label was sewn into the outer sacking; and on it was printed WESTMINSTER UNITED CHURCH WINNIPEG. It was part of the first bundle our women had contributed to CCRA.

And no one had a camera.

The *Hilfswerk* people kept me on an exacting schedule. But in Heidelberg they took me to see Maryann Meyer-Kramer.

She and her husband were both waiting for my coming, and though we had only part of one afternoon we had a delightful visit. They gave me coffee, from a Westminster CARE parcel, and bread with butter also from Westminster. They told me how with the coming of Canadian food and vitamins both of them had recovered remarkably in health. They were rid of the unrelieved tiredness with which they had gone to work each morning.

They also took me to meet Mrs. Karl Goerdeler who lived nearby. She was probably well on in her sixties. She had once been the first lady of Leipzig. Now, with a servant in a tiny farm cottage, she was trying to grow a few extra potatoes for the winter.

The visit to the Goerdelers was the highlight of my journey. The next morning I started back for Amsterdam, whence I flew to Glasgow where Esther was waiting with a friend of ours from Union Seminary days.

From Glasgow, we went to Edinburgh to visit other friends, including Dr. Hugh Watt, under whom I had written my thesis. Then we went on down to England where at Bradford we visited the girl who lived with us during the war, Marjorie Newton (her brother John was away at sea). Marjorie was living with her parents. For the first time, we had the pleasure of meeting them in person.

Our return to Winnipeg dumped us into a flurry of activities, winding up our last weeks at Westminster. Moving is an enterprise which, like marriage, is not to be taken in hand lightly or thoughtlessly—nor without immense reserves of muscle and patience. We went through that huge three-story house of ours and had most of the packing done before the paid movers came in.

In addition, to provide some report of the memorable events to which the Westminster congregation had so generously sent us, I had to preach special sermons, and both Esther and I had to give talks to interested groups elsewhere.

Then came the farewell events with their warm tributes and good wishes, in the expression of which kindness and sympathy overcame any honest impulse to dull affairs by pointing out that no one could be that good—except at a funeral.

In any case, if some lewd fellow of the baser sort had attempted to exploit the opportunity by quoting the Scripture, "woe unto you when all men speak well of you," I was effectively insulated from that doom. No one could have taken as clear stands as I had on so many controversial issues without creating foes. I was aware that some in Winnipeg would regard my departure as a public improvement. But one must be measured in part by the enemies one makes. I felt an enormous reservoir of good will in the Westminster congregation and in Winnipeg itself.

I was content.

In the pulpit of the newly rebuilt Bloor St. United Church.
My admonitions, still in the gown that George Hormel gave me,
were directed to an empty building,
under the direction of a photographer as the sole audience.

Chapter 15

Toronto

*Shakespeare
and a church on fire*

Early in November, in weather almost as chilly as it was on that October when we brought Margery to Winnipeg, our family, including our spaniel Sparkie, crowded into our well-worn Plymouth and headed out for Toronto, our goods and chattels following in more leisurely stages by rail. Once more we had passed a great divide.

My move to Bloor Street had one immediate consequence. At a single stroke, I had cut the cords of all the committees, projects and offices with which in Winnipeg I had progressively become involved. This was all to the good. I was free, as I had not been for years, to concentrate on the work of my own congregation. I had also the further advantage that Dr. Pidgeon's associate, the Rev. Preston Macleod, stayed with me for the best part of my first year. His knowledge of every aspect of the church's work, his tact in dealing with the congregation, and his warm friendliness to me smoothed my way remarkably.

I was further fortunate that after Preston had gone I was able to recruit another gifted young man, the Rev. Kenneth Cleator, who had been my assistant in Winnipeg during the war years. It had been owing to the competence of Cleator and of his successor, the Rev. Reid Vipond, that the work of Westminster Church had been so well managed, while so heavy a share of my time was diverted to outside obligations. The two men had different gifts, but they both had great competence. Throughout my ministry I have been lucky beyond my deserving in having as assistants younger men who had talents that I did not possess.

I came to Toronto at a time when churches everywhere needed new ventures to break through old conventions. In the war years many of the peace-time programs had to give place to the immediate necessities of national service. When the war was over churches had new problems and needed new directives.

As an instance, in the late 40s, one of the most pressing tasks confronting Bloor Street Church was that of aiding in such ways as we could the successive waves of New Canadians who had begun to stream across the Atlantic to come to Canada, most to Toronto.

For awhile we dealt with Baltic peoples. The National Baltic celebration, now held annually in commemoration of those killed by the Communists, was in its first years held in Bloor Street Church.

Following the Baltic groups came new streams; Hungarians, Italians, Germans, and companies from Great Britain. We tried to make them all feel that no matter what their nationality or religion, the United Church was eager to help. We made use of our rooms—some for classes in English, some for social gatherings.

In our own congregation, we initiated a variety of different programs: A Campus Club for university students (a club which continued for 20 years); a Young Singles Club, a Young Adults Club; a Married Couples Club; and a Men's Club, meeting for dinner and a speaker (which also continued for upward of 20 years). I also started publication of a congregational paper: *The Church Tower*. All these were in addition to a number of organizations (mostly for women) already established.

I continued to give a great deal of time to the preparation of sermons. During my first winter I started a series on "Parables in Plays." My first venture was with Shakespeare. After an initial sermon on the historic relation of drama to religion I dealt, on successive Sunday evenings, with moral issues in the great Tragedies: *Hamlet, Othello, King Lear* and *Macbeth*. In a following year I picked up the idea again and had another series on *Richard III, Julius Caesar, The Merchant of Venice* and *The Tempest*. When I had finished the second series I sent the text of both to Abingdon Press, which published them in a book entitled *Spiritual Values in Shakespeare*. After the hard-cover edition was sold out, Abingdon reprinted the text as a paperback, and sold it in the U.S. for several years.

I received reviews of *Spiritual Values* from all over the continent, most of them highly flattering. But because it came from home I liked best of all that of Robertson Davies in *Saturday Night*. After saying

176

that "if this is the kind of thing Dr. Howse is giving to the young people of his flock, they are lucky indeed," he compared the book to four other Shakespeare books written by Shakespearian scholars and said, "I do not think that any of these people (some of whom are famous) get any farther than Dr. Howse, and they are not nearly so modest."

The praise was not as lavish as that of some others; but considering the source, it was more gratifying.

In subsequent years, I gave two more series on modern plays, ranging from Browning's *Pippa Passes* to Christopher Fry's *Sleep of Prisoners* and Gratien Gelinas' *Ti-Coq*. I had begun arrangement for having these plays published in a book similar to *Spiritual Values*. But the former manager of the publishing house retired; the new manager was lukewarm about such books, and the project fell through. I still have the typescript for the series.

In the morning services I began three series (seven sermons each) of a different kind. They gave a systematic, historical survey of Old Testament literature. I picked up two series that I had delivered in Winnipeg and had published as two paper-back booklets. When I completed the survey, Allen and Unwin of London published all three in one book, *The Lively Oracles*.

Again I received most gratifying reviews, not only from all across Canada but from overseas, in papers ranging from the *London Times*, to the *Bombay Times,* India.

But I made a mistake in giving books to two different publishers. Neither would promote the books of the other. In consequence *The Lively Oracles* was never sold in the U.S.; and *Spiritual Values* was never sold in England.

I also prepared studies on Biblical characters; on the reformers Wycliffe, Hus, Luther, Knox; on a variety of other notables ranging to Augustine and Socrates; and on The Divine Light in Literature: studies on such masterpieces as *Les Miserables*. I am sorry that I never did get these prepared for publishing. Had I done so I would

the flames
shot thirty feet
through the roof

have had more for my labours than I have left today.

One formidable task left as a legacy of war was the need for extensive renovation of the church buildings. In 1940, the Bloor Street congregation, with daring and wisdom, had built a new Assembly Hall. But the rest of the structure was old. And in the stringency of wartime, repairs were of necessity neglected. We faced a heavy backlog of deferred maintenance.

We made plans for progressive restoration. We took as one of our first jobs the renovation of the sanctuary. As one detail, we took out every square inch of the stained glass, and had the design refashioned and rebuilt with an admixture of new glass. The total effect was to increase immeasurably the attractiveness of the windows.

Another venture brought more divided response. We changed the immemorial dark brown of the interior and the pews to a very light pastel green. The majority of the congregation seemed to approve; but some thought it next to sacrilege. One indignant lady asked me whether we were going to put a bar in the vestibule.

We did not know the futility of our efforts. The final details of painting were done in the summer of 1954; but most of the congregation never saw the completed job.

The last paint cans had not been carried away, when on the night of August 30 the newly refurbished sanctuary went up in flames.

Bloor Street Church is really a collection of different buildings. Though the flames were frightening as they shot twenty or thirty feet through the roof, the firemen were able to contain the fire. They saved the section at the rear containing the Assembly Hall, the Chapel, the class rooms and the Ladies Club room—not to mention the indispensible kitchen. But the Sanctuary was gutted and open to the sky—destroyed. Our beautiful rebuilt windows, alas, were all gone.

The stone walls still stood, held in place (as would have been impossible for steel) by 12 by 12 wooden rafters. Some of them, despite the hours of fire, were not burned through; enough of them to keep the wall in place, and save the building. Ironically no such construction is possible today.

One memorable coincidence marked the morning of the fire. Bloor Street had just engaged a new assistant minister, the Rev. Walter (Paddy) Sellars, to follow Ken Cleator who was leaving. Sellars was on his way by automobile to Toronto but had detoured to St. Catherines to visit some friends. While I was down at the scene of the fire, lugging to safety such items as I wished to spare from possible danger, Esther phoned Paddy. He hustled his family into his car and arrived in time to see the church where he was supposed to begin work the next day still smouldering defiance to the hoses.

Paddy, as the congregation would soon learn, was a young man of sundry and superlative talents. I sensed that he was not dismayed but excited. To him a disaster was a great field for operations.

The fire immensely increased my work during the next couple of years. We decided without hesitation not to move to another site. At the height of the fire when I was hurrying across the street trying to salvage some objects of value, a reporter asked me what we were going to do. I replied, "We shall rebuild." Suggestions were made that we cash in on the impressive value of our real estate (frontage on two streets and 35,000 square feet of land), combine it with the substantial sum of our insurance and move to some desirable location in the suburbs. But the church officials unanimously endorsed the decision to stay where we were. We did send a committee to visit our two neighbouring churches, Trinity and Avenue Road, to propose that we pool the resources of the three congregations to build one centre for the United Church in that area. But we got nowhere with that proposal and we decided to go it alone.

We were fortunate that the University of Toronto, through its President Sidney Smith, a friend of mine since Dalhousie days and a Bloor Street elder, offered us the use of Convocation Hall for our Sunday morning services. For the Sunday evenings we joined with our neighbour, Trinity United Church.

In the long run, the fire was a blessing in disguise. The new interior of the sanctuary was an immense improvement on the old and the new windows, later crowned by the Great South window above the gallery, are a treasure for the church, the city and the nation.

The Great South window was, I believe, the first window in the world to commemorate the ecumenical movement. The faces and figures in its panels were inspired by photography that I took at the first two Assemblies of the World Council of Churches. Men from far countries, had they chanced to enter Bloor Street Church, could have looked up and seen themselves.

On January 8, 1956, a year and a half after the fire, we had the rededication service for the restored building. It was an inspiring hour. The congregation had a new spring in its step, a new light in its eye, and a new hope in its heart. I ended the dedication sermon with a quotation from "Hudson's Last Voyage":

> "We'll keep the honour of a certain aim
> Amid the peril of uncertain waves
> And sail ahead and leave the rest to God."

Chapter 16:

Christians and Muslims

*hearing God's voice
through other ears*

1954 was not only "the year of the fire." Before that morning in August it had already brought two important events—one of extraordinary nature.

Not long after the New Year, I received a letter from Garland Evans Hopkins, an editor of perhaps the most widely read and influential religious periodical of the time, *The Christian Century* of Chicago. He wrote to tell me of a remarkable convocation being planned for the Middle East. A number of churchmen, scholars, diplomats and others had been working for a long time to raise the funds and to seek throughout the world the cooperation necessary to organize a meeting between distinguished leaders of two great religious communities separated by the enmity of more than a thousand years, Christianity and Islam.

The gathering was planned to meet in April in Bhamdoun, Lebanon. An extraordinarily distinguished group of about 25 Muslim religious leaders, representing centres of Islamic life from Africa to Indonesia, had agreed to come.

A similar number of Christians had also agreed. They were not coming as nominees of their churches. At that time many if not most Christian churches would not nominate anyone to discuss religion with men whom they regarded as "heathen." The church leaders, clerical and lay, were coming as individuals selected by the organizing committee. Acceptances had already come from the four great stems of Christian history: Coptic, Orthodox, Roman Catholic and Protestant.

The convocation was designed to open communication between representatives of the Christian and Muslim faiths, and to explore the possibility of developing a relationship more worthy of the best heritage of both.

All this was astonishing to me; but nothing was more astonishing than the conclusion of the letter, which invited me to be the Canadian representative of the twenty-five Christians invited from throughout the world.

I had one possible explanation as to why I was included in that select company. I had been for some years a correspondent of the *Christian Century*. And, though I had never before had direct contact with Hopkins, I must have profited from the draw in the lottery of his mind.

Early in April, I flew to the Middle East. It was the first time I had crossed the Atlantic by air, and on that memorable night I did not even attempt to sleep. We were flying above unbroken banks of cloud, and above us was the unscreened resplendence of a full moon. In the reflected light the surface of the clouds seemed not like clouds but rather like an Arctic landscape of solid snow, over which a Captain Scott might perchance be seen plodding toward the Pole.

I reflected that when I was born, no human being since the beginning of time had ever been able to look upon the splendid vestment of Mother Earth as I was seeing it now; and that the humblest traveller by air now could peer from his little window on aspects of terrestrial grandeur that none of the great ones of the past from Galileo to Plato had ever been able even to imagine.

The convocation in Bhamdoun, a few miles outside Beirut, was a memorable affair. At that time, the idea that Christians and Muslims could seriously talk to each other about the mutual issues of their faith seemed to both Christians and Muslims of conservative stripe an outrage. However, we had some impressive backers. When the convocation opened the sheaf of goodwill telegrams from distinguished individuals in many countries included those from the Prime Minister of Pakistan and from Albert Schweitzer in Africa.

In Bhamdoun, I received an education that I could not have equalled in all the books I could read in a lifetime. I met and listened to scholarly leaders from different lands in the far flung Islamic world, as they talked, argued, and at times engaged in their prayers.

I especially remember one devout sheik, a professor in an Islamic university, then coming to the end of his career. His prayers seemed to me similar to those of my Methodist father.

Later I was to have the privilege of being host to that teacher when

182

some predicted
the meeting would collapse
in hostility and suspicion

he came on a tour to the West. I even had him preach on Sunday evening in Bloor Street Church. This was, I believe, the first time in Canadian history that a Muslim Imam preached (though through an interpreter) from a Christian pulpit.

One ironic feature of the venture: not only was this the first occasion in more than 1400 years of religious history when representatives of Islam sat down around a common table with their Christian counterparts, to talk of their faith. This was also the first occasion when the four branches of the Christian faith—Coptic, Orthodox, Roman Catholic and Protestant—had even made such a venture among themselves.

Cynics said that it was more remarkable for the Christians to get together than it was to have them meet the Muslims.

Despite the cynics, the convocation altogether was a success, almost beyond expectations. Just as when the World Council of Churches was founded in Amsterdam some observers predicted that the enterprise would collapse in mutual animosities, so some predicted that the Muslim-Christian meeting would collapse in hostility and suspicion. Instead there came from all sections of the gathering an amazed appreciation that they were not the only ones interested in peace and good will. The assembled delegates discovered a mutual desire for cooperation greater than either company had believed possible in the other.

At the conclusion of the convocation the delegates, without a dissenting voice, affirmed that cooperation between their two monotheistic faiths was not only possible but desirable. They constituted themselves as the Continuing Committee On Muslim-Christian Cooperation and elected from their number an executive board of thirty-two to plan a worldwide organization somewhat patterned on the World Council of Churches.

I was one of those elected to the Committee's executive, and so in February 1955 I went to its first meeting in Alexandria, Egypt. There a group of us spent a strenuous week drafting a constitution which

we did not know the forces which would strangle the "noble experiment"

would also serve provisionally as the founding constitution of a permanent organization to be called the World Fellowship of Muslims and Christians. For the interim the executive elected a slate of officers to head the Continuing Committee in its formidable task of bringing into being the proposed World Fellowship.

The Constitution Committee had chosen me as its Chairman and I had presided over sessions where sometimes the reasoning and the assumptions, not to mention the prejudices, became prickly. I had not kept in contact with progress in other departments. I was dumbfounded when, just before the committee on nominations was to present its report, Hopkins informed me that I was slated as the Christian Co-chairman.

For this I was not prepared. Compared to many of the distinguished scholars in the company, some of whom were fluent in both English and Arabic, I was an amateur.

I let Hopkins have my vigorous objection. We had a long conversation. I soon learned that my nomination had little to do with intrinsic qualifications. It was a matter of politics. It was unwise to pick an American. The convocation was being attacked as a hidden enterprise of the State Department. It was unwise to elect an Englishman. The Suez occupation had left hostilities still smouldering. Among all the delegates, the one who would be most conveniently in touch with New York, where the operation would be directed, was a Canadian. Any other Canadian who had happened to be there would have been elected, as I was. Nevertheless I counted it an honour to have been elected, and in succeeding days tried to exercise in a credible manner my stints as chairman of the plenary sessions.

At the close of its Alexandria sessions, the Continuing Committee on Muslim-Christian Cooperation, now established with an adopted constitution, authorized its new officers to proceed with plans for the permanent organization.

The prospects looked good. Like King David of old we could hear "the sound of a going in the tops of the mulberry trees." Alas, we did not know the strength of forces both in the West and in the Middle East which would strangle the "noble experiment" at its birth.

There were two causes of the early death of this extraordinary beginning.

The first was lack of money. Some special gifts funded the initial meetings; but to keep the movement going required substantial capital consistently available. The Muslim-Christian cause fell between two stools. On the one hand the large American foundations would not support it because it was a religious enterprise. On the other hand, the sources of religious funds, the large denominations and the World Council of Churches for example, would not support it because at that time most Christian leaders looked upon any attempt to talk seriously to other faiths as a sure road to syncretism. When he had used up the first substantial grant Hopkins began a losing battle. Time might have brought new supporters; but time was lacking.

The second cause of collapse was political. John Foster Dulles, then American Secretary of State wielding the big stick in Middle East diplomacy, withdrew American support for the Aswan Dam in Egypt. His bellicose act infuriated the peoples of the Middle East. Some of our strongest Muslim supporters advised us that the policies of the Western nations had changed the mental climate and that any Muslim-Christian venture would have to wait for a better day.

Almost thirty years have passed but that better day has not yet dawned. Indeed the storm clouds are more lurid now than they were then.

Shortly after I had been elected Co-chairman I heard a broadcast in Arabic which friends told me was a bitter denunciation of me as pro-Israeli. Somehow over there someone knew all about my activity in the Canadian Council of Christians and Jews. They deduced that I was at least a Zionist in disguise, and probably a hireling of the Americans.

To balance this, when I came back to Toronto I was denounced by some as anti-semitic, because I had been dealing with Arabs. I received quite a spate of hate mail and telephone calls, some in the middle of the night, and some even suggesting that the caller would be looking for my name in the obituary columns. At that time, and even now, it is difficult to deal with either party without being suspect by the other.

One last addendum: Our Alexandria meeting gave me some interesting contacts with a young man named Anwar Sadat. Anwar El

Sadat was the way it was written then. When we landed at Cairo before moving to Alexandria, a great deal of hostile comment greeted our coming. The opposition was fanned by the Grand Mufti, who in wartime had been a strong pro-Nazi.

However the strings were pulled, Hopkins on landing found himself in real trouble. He could not get the convocation material through customs. He found the hotel cancelling reservations. He had telephone calls from certain officials begging to be excused from the opening dinner. Altogether he was in a fix.

Someone suggested to us that a good man to see would be Anwar Sadat, second in command to Egyptian president Col. Nasser. We telephoned Sadat, got through at once, had a cordial reception and an invitation to come on over to his office.

Immediately on our arrival he came to the door to meet us. He was then about in his middle thirties, a handsome young man, smartly dressed. He asked us about our work and assured us that he was heartily in favour of what we were doing; that he was sorry for our trouble, and that he would watch our progress with interest.

Almost by magic everything changed. The customs were helpful, the hotels were courteous, and the official who couldn't come to the banquet found that he was free after all.

When the Alexandria conference was over and I had been elected Christian Co-chairman, on my return to Cairo, Sadat got in touch with me and invited me to be his guest for such time as I could spare. I stayed for four days. Sadat paid my hotel bill and every day sent me an army car with a driver, and on two occasions a professor of history, to show me around Egypt.

When I had returned to Toronto and sent Col. Sadat my bread-and-butter thank you, he replied. He said that I was thanking him only for something he felt "a duty towards you as a brother and a man of culture." Then he added, "Truly I am glad to know you and I hope to see you again in the future. Awaiting to hear the best of you I remain ..."

That letter was dated May 1955. When Christmas came I received from Sadat a Christmas card, and in 1956 again I received from him a Christmas card.

To my great regret, somehow when I was cleaning my church office I misplaced these two cards. But I still have his letter and I intend to keep it as a momento of an extraordinary man.

The other important outside event in 1954 was the holding in

it bogged down
in lugubrious
intrusions

August in Evanston, Illinois of the second Assembly of the World
Council of Churches. (I just got home from the event in time for the
fire.)

I had enjoyed so much the first Assembly in Amsterdam and
profited so greatly by being there, that I decided to attend the second
Assembly. As it would be frustrating just to be present only as a
casual outsider, I arranged with the Toronto *Star* to have accreditation as a news correspondent. I wrote a front-page story for the
opening day and further dispatches throughout the sessions.

This was of some help in meeting expenses. But that was secon-
dary. I became aware that the most profitable way to attend such a
gathering was as a representative of the Press. At any given time, a
delegate had to be in his own allotted place, working at his particular
sub-committee or his routine denominational assignment.

But a newspaper correspondent could choose to be where the action was. He needed no introduction to speak to anybody, delegate,
official, or invading critic.

And he had another immeasurable advantage. The World Council
made provision for news media which were, I am told, markedly
superior to those of the Vatican Councils. They provided each ac-
creditated correspondent with an ample mailbox. Every morning,
and repeatedly through the day, that box would be supplied with the
text (in advance) of every speech, the report of every committee, the
minutes of the preceding session, the drafts of proposed motions or
amendments, and all the vital documents of the daily Assembly.

Further, the representatives of the news media had the advantage
of daily briefing sessions and press conferences which rigorously
questioned controversial speakers, officials or critics. The Press
Card provided an extraordinary Open Sesame to whatever of worth
the Assembly contained.

From Evanston on I resolved to make the most of it.

Looking back, I judge Evanston the least inspiring of all of the
five Assemblies so far held. Despite its theme, The Hope of the
World, it bogged down from time to time in lugubrious intrusions of

Neo-Orthodox theology. Despite this, however, Evanston had its solid achievements. It had a magnificent night of drama in Chicago's Soldier's Field, and profited rather than suffered from the daily barrage of acrimony in the Chicago *Tribune*.

Evanston had no high moment of emotion to match the opening service in the Neiuwe Kerk at Amsterdam. But it was significant that at the close it picked up the Amsterdam council's final affirmation, "We Intend To Stay Together," and added, "To Stay Together Is Not Enough; We Must Grow Together."

As a consequence of that second event in 1954, I was later able to attend other World Council Assemblies. The third Assembly was held in 1961 in Asia, in Delhi, India. I attended that as the special correspondent of the Toronto *Telegram*. The most portentous event of that Assembly was the reception of the enormous Orthodox delegation from Russia. This, together with the reception of something like a dozen new churches from Africa and others from Third World Countries, changed the political balance of the council.

At its founding the World Council, though geographically a world organization, was largely representative of Europe and America. Though it included delegates from both Coptic and Orthodox churches, it could be classed as pan-Protestantism. With the inclusion of the delegations received in New Delhi, the churches of America and Europe could for the first time be a minority. The pattern of the World Council of Churches took on in some degree the pattern of the United Nations—with some similar consequences.

When the 1961 Assembly was over I did not come immediately home. I had already taken time to visit the Taj Mahal—one of the few sights of the world that is impossible to overestimate. I went north to the Punjab and the city of Ludhiana, to visit some of our missionaries, and thence on to the new city of Chundigar at the foot of the Himalayas.

On leaving India, I did not turn back but kept on eastwards to Singapore (where I stayed at the famous Raffles Hotel) and from thence to Hong Kong, at that time the most exciting marketplace in the world, the place where everybody went broke saving money. From Hong Kong I went on to Japan, Honolulu and Los Angeles and Toronto. For someone who was born before an aeroplane had ever flown, it was quite a trip.

The fourth Assembly, in 1968, was held in Uppsala, Sweden. Again I reported for the Toronto *Telegram*. This was the first time I

188

used the marvellous efficiency of Telex.

The distinctive feature of this assembly was the changed relationship with the Roman Catholic Church. At the Amsterdam Assembly the Pope forbade Roman Catholics to attend. At Evanston, the Roman Catholic Archbishop of Chicago approved the attendance only of individuals who had business there. At New Delhi, the Pope sent observers. But at Uppsala, the leading speech was given by a Roman Catholic, Barbara Ward, Lady Jackson. Another keynote address was given by a priest sent as representative of the Pope. And a strong group of Roman Catholic scholars was appointed to the Theological Commission of the World Council. From Amsterdam to Uppsala was a considerable journey.

The fifth Assembly was held in 1975 in Africa; in Nairobi, Kenya. By that time I had retired, and for five years had been writing a weekly column in the Toronto *Star*. The *Star* sent me to Nairobi, not this time with the exacting task of writing daily reports; but simply to observe and keep myself informed.

If any single feature marked the Nairobi Assembly it was the intense drive spearheaded by Third World representatives to involve the World Council in social and political action. One of the chief speakers was premier Michael Manly of Jamaica. Much of the World Council's later involvement in liberation movements had birth in the Nairobi Assembly.

I could attend all these great events only because I was writing for daily newspapers. Most of the people who were delegates had been present at only one Assembly. I was the only Canadian present at them all. In the Press gallery at Nairobi I was moved to reflect that I was perhaps the only newspaper man and one of the very few people in the whole world who could listen to the debates and relate them to memories of what all other Assemblies had done, in all the previous sessions since Amsterdam.

I had one last legacy from the five Assemblies. From Evanston on I collected and preserved all the important documents that came to my press box day by day. At the close of each Assembly I would parcel them and send them by sea mail back home. It seems hardly possible that there can be any other such collection in Canada. At the time of my retirement, I sent them all down to the United Church Archives, where, I hope, they may be of use to future students of World Council Assemblies.

Margery on her wedding day.
The Rev. Kenneth Cleator and I officiated.
I was attired in the splendour of the moderatorial stole and vest,
with a Litt. D. hood from Memorial University, Newfoundland.

190

Chapter 17:

Moderator

*leading a church
and raising a storm*

However busy my days may have been in normal times—if I had any normal times—none were busier than those in the two years, 1964-66, when I was Moderator of the United Church of Canada.

(Moderator of the United Church, by the way, is the correct title, *not* Moderator of the General Council. See Record of Proceedings, Kingston General Council, 1968).

My references to outside activities which claimed my attention and took my time may have tended to obscure the fact that all through my ministry I tried to be a good churchman. I went faithfully to Presbytery and Conference. I took an active part in the proceedings. In Winnipeg I had been chairman of Presbytery, and in Toronto I had been President of Conference, and given a good deal of that year to visiting presbyteries, especially those in the north. I had also been on a steady stream of United Church Committees of various sorts, and held office in such organizations as the Lord's Day Alliance, the Temperance Society and the Bible Society. Also, beginning in 1942, I had been elected as Commissioner to seven General Councils. I was familiar with the ways of ecclesiastical tribunals.

But serving as Moderator—the highest office in the church—is different from serving in these other offices. It is really a full time job for two full years, and has unique obligations and rewards.

It happened that in 1964 the biennial General Council of the United Church met in Canada's newest province, Newfoundland. I had been elected a Commissioner to that Council, and as Esther had so far seen Newfoundland only in such distant and fleeting glimpses as were possible from passenger steamers, passing north or south on their way across the Atlantic, we decided to go early and spend some time touring that land of my forebears.

Our headquarters were in St. John's, at the home of my brother Claude, the only one of our immediate family still living on our native island. But we had hardly arrived when I was laid low with some obnoxious virus from which I recovered barely in time to make it to the opening session of General Council, at which the Moderator was to be elected.

In the United Church, Moderatorial elections have frequently been long drawn-out ordeals. With half a dozen or more nominees in the running, each ballot eliminated only the man with the lowest vote. Then another vote would have to be taken.

On this occasion, the Council was spared that tribulation. A substantial number of ministers and laymen had been nominated—nine I think, including several Newfoundlanders—but one after another had dropped out. When the balloting began, only three nominees remained on the list. They were: The Rev. Dr. Alex Kerr, sometime Principal of Pine Hill, and former President of Dalhousie University; The Rev. Dr. Elias Andrews, Principal of Queens Theological College, another Newfoundlander; and I. All of us had been friends since college days.

When I was elected on the first ballot the other two graciously moved that the Council make the election unanimous.

It was for me a pleasant co-incidence that the Council was held in Gower Street Church, the church in which, forty years earlier, I had been received—not without some misgiving from my examining elders—as a candidate for the Methodist ministry.

My election suddenly brought an enormous accretion to my responsibilities. Since the Moderatorship was a temporary appointment I did not choose to resign from the pastorate of Bloor Street Church. Fortunately now as in other critical periods of my ministry I was able to count on a competent assistant. Cleator and Sellars had been followed by Stan Kennedy, an experienced and resourceful pastor who had given special study to the art of counselling, and Ben Zinck a sensitive, attractive young man from Nova Scotia. Just prior to my election I had employed as assistant a multi-talented individual, Donald Gillies. And I had as visiting minister the Rev. Fred Baine, a man whose rare graciousness of spirit would be an unfailing asset in every time of trouble. Nevertheless, in my new office I would be immediately faced with a new and massive dimension of duties.

In the United Church order of government, which is a heritage from both Presbyterian and Methodist patterns of administration, the Moderatorship is not just a ceremonial office. The church's constitution states categorically that the Moderator is "the chief executive officer of the church." A Moderator has to preside not only over those interminable sessions of the Council which elects him or her, but also over the continuing meetings of the Executive, the Sub-executive and, if necessary the Judicial committee. Moreover, the Moderator is *ex-officio* a member of *all* the Divisions and Committees of the church. Nothing is outside his or her purview.

But the most awesome of responsibilities go beyond those of administration. The Moderator's duties, as laid down, among others, in the Manual, are "To give leadership to the church, especially in spiritual things" and "To visit throughout the church, giving sympathetic guidance and counsel in all its affairs."

Such a commission could daunt anyone.

For me the pressure began as soon as I had adjourned the Council assembly and went to the news room. There they were—the retinue of Press, Radio and TV. Some of them I knew and had jousted with before. All of them wanted something which would at least be quotable, and if possible shocking. I tried then, as I habitually had in public statements, not to evade any legitimate question, but so far as my knowledge went to give my reply honestly and clearly. In return, I can after many years report that with few exceptions the media representatives reported me responsibly and fairly.

*If my memory serves me,
this was on Moderatorial travels
with Dr. Francis Ibiam
of Nigeria.*

193

However, because I had been for many years identified with issues (not to mention opinions and beliefs) which had attracted a good deal of media attention, I started willy-nilly as what our modern jargon calls a "high profile" Moderator.

Within a short period after my election I had been the subject of feature articles in two then current magazines, the *Star Weekly* and the *Globe Magazine*. I had been presented in a TV program of the *Heritage* series; Profile of a Moderator. I had been the mystery guest on *Front Page Challenge* on TV, and I had been commended— sometimes with reservations—in an impressive number of newspaper articles and editorials. And as I began to travel throughout Canada, I was on a continual parade of newspaper, radio and TV interviews and talk shows.

As time went on, explosions of publicity accompanied certain episodes. The most notable of these came when I said during one Easter season that I did not believe in the physical resurrection of Jesus. (For this I had good company in St. Paul.) The barrage of public controversy unleashed by this statement (about as radical as an affirmation that the world is round) was incredible. Some newspapers had a field day. I was away from Toronto (in Montreal, I think) when the story broke. I got telephone calls asking me, protentously, if the stories were true. Somebody even got Billy Graham, then on some mission in Vancouver, to reach half across a continent and rebuke me with a solemn admonition.

The letters to the editor which came to newspapers were matched by those which came to me. Some writers fired off with words such as Atheist, Godless, Emissary of Satan. Others, more in sorrow than in anger, assured me that they would be praying for me. One voluble lady after a mixed brew of biblical exposition and personal vituperation ended with a last satisfying reflection: "I hear that you do not believe in Hell. Sir! You are in for a surprise."

Meanwhile, I had the routine legitimate obligations of a Moderator, including a mathematically impossible number of invitations: to be the speaker at congregational anniversaries; at high school graduations; to dedicate some new church or old folks home; to take Lenten services; to attend, and sometimes to speak at, university convocations—the uncovenanted rewards of which were four more doctoral degrees *Honoris Causa;* and, in the course of the Church Union debate, to speak a muted word in a rich assortment of meetings designated by that blessed word "dialogue."

a single-engined plane
in a snowstorm—
the engine conked out

During the course of my two years I visited all of the United Church's eleven regional Conferences, making speeches at every stop. As 1965 was the fortieth anniversary of our church, I gave several special addresses in celebration of that milestone. I visited also a number of Presbyteries and women's Presbyterials and home mission fields, on travels which took me from the outports of Newfoundland and the interior of Labrador to the mission station at Oxford House, near Hudson's Bay, and to the shores of British Columbia.

As we left Oxford House in a single-engined plane in a snow storm at a time when temperatures had been down to 60 degrees below zero, Fahrenheit, the engine conked out. We slumped downwards but after some seconds the pilot, switching on the spare tank of gas, managed to get a spit, a cough, and at last the old familiar hum. Inside the little plane nobody said a single word for some time after. I think that I broke the silence by saying, "I like that new sound."

In addition to the church engagements there were civic, provincial and national affairs. There were trips to Ottawa: to meet the Queen, to attend the opening of Parliament, to have a State dinner and reception at Government House, to have a private dinner with the Governor General and Mrs. Vanier, to attend the national service of mourning for Winston Churchill. And there were affairs in Ontario such as the opening of the Provincial Parliament, and others.

Along with these occasions came one more special than all the others—in July, 1965, in Bloor Street Church, the marriage of my only daughter, Margery Joan to Raymond Dyer, a high school teacher of languages, for whom we had formed a high regard that has grown over the years. That was the highlight of my two years.

However crowded my Canadian schedule may have been, I had a strong concern, which I had affirmed at the time of my election, to reinforce in our church the perception of its responsibilities in our mission fields throughout the world. I had always considered our missionaries to be the pioneers of Christianity and the most effective witnesses of its evangel. I also had at times the feeling that the contact between our missionaries, often in lonely and unpleasant places, and the rest of us, so comfortable in the home church, left much to be desired.

I decided therefore to do something to reassure our representatives in mission fields that they held the place of honour as our vanguard troops. I thought that a visit from the Moderator to the workers in the mission fields might do something to convey the warm good will of their fellow Christians at home.

In two years I could visit all the Conferences in Canada; but I could not visit all the operating centres of our Division of World Outreach, as our missionary program is presently called. I decided that I could attempt to visit our missionaries in the Caribbean and South America, and later those in the Far East. That would be the most I could do.

I decided also that as most of the missionaries whom we should be meeting, and in whose homes we should be entertained, would be missionaries with spouses, so the visit should be not only of the Moderator but of the Moderator and his wife. The missionary family, as distinct from the group of males or females, has been the distinctive mark of Protestant evangelism. But too often that family in some isolated outpost has been visited only by the male executive. Wives, too, can get lonely; and the talk in the kitchen may be as important as the sermon from the pulpit.

In July 1965, a week after Margery's wedding, Esther and I set out for the Caribbean and South America, to survey the programs in which our missionaries there were working.

First we went to Jamaica where we spent a brief but well planned

---

I asked
if there were any sharks
in the area.
"Not often," he said.
"Usually you can see their fins."

few days. We had a meeting with the Synod and visited schools and churches, and had a constant and pleasant succession of lunch and dinner engagements. On Sunday the regular service of worship was held at 7:30 in the morning—it was cooler then. Among our hosts were the Rev. Neil Banks, who a few years before had been in our young people's group at Bloor Street, and Fred Whiting, a business man who had been in our Actimist Club in Westminster Church, Winnipeg.

From Jamaica, we went to Trinidad, where the Presbyterian Church from its inception has been associated with the Canadian Church. There our program was organized by such Trinidadians as Senator Roy Neehall, who used to attend Bloor Street, the Rev. Jim Seunarine, who later came to serve the United Church in Toronto, and the Rev. Albert Baldeo, who, with his Canadian wife, is now a minister in Kelowna, B.C.

Again we had a series of engagements, receptions, inspections of schools, a visit with the local synod and so on. In one place I turned the sod for a new church.

We still had time for picnics and swims. On one of our swims I asked our host if there were any sharks in the area.

He said, "Not often."

I asked, "How do you know when they are here?"

"Usually you can see their fins," he replied.

It struck me that this occasion might be unusual. I ended my swim with an abruptness which I hoped was not too obvious.

Leaving Trinidad we flew over the impenetrable Amazon basin to Rio de Janerio. Our visit there happened to co-incide with the 400th anniversary of Brazil.

In Rio we spent some time seeing both the splendor of the scenery and the squalor of the favelas. We visited a variety of social service agencies, all of them with their resources overwhelmed by the need.

Then the Rev. Don Raffan, one of our United Church ministers and also an agricultural specialist, arrived to take us on a two-day drive in a VW bus to the remote rural area where he was then working. We travelled over the worst and most dangerous roads (so called) I have ever seen, and learned that rural poverty can be, if anything, more deadly than urban poverty.

On the Sunday I was staying with the Raffans, as a pleasant personal contact in the routine of official travel, I baptised the Raffan's first baby. After some further time looking at the work Raffan was doing to teach poverty stricken farmers better methods of agriculture, we jumped by a skimpy little air-taxi to Belo Horizonte, and thence to Dourados where we were met by another United Church of Canada couple, the Rev. Tom and Rita Edmonds. Tom had special competence in the problems of urban poverty. He and Rita were our pleasant and hospitable hosts while we got further education in the social complexities of Brazil. Then we went south to Santa Maria, where we were met by another Canadian couple, Vernon and Betty Lou Hutson. Vernon, a native of Barbados, had first studied agriculture and then theology. He too was trying to relieve chronic poverty by the introduction of better methods of farming. Like other missionaries, the Hutsons impressed me as exceptional people. They were all dedicating technical competence with rare and noble spirit.

I cannot here report with more than sketchy reference, those weeks of travel and those enlightening visits. When we left Brazil we went on first to Buenos Aires, Argentina, and then to Santiago, Chile. In both of these cities I discussed with the leading Methodist bishops the possibility, of which then they had some hope, that the United Church of Canada might be able to send them missionaries like those in Brazil with special technical training.

When we turned around to go home, we flew first to Lima, Peru, where we took time off to visit the wonders of the Inca remains at Cuzco, (crossing mountain ranges of more than 20,000 feet). Another flight took us on to Panama—for another brief visit—and thence to Miami and Toronto.

It had been quite a trip, and to me quite a revelation of the nature of missionary enterprise in the modern day.

In September, Esther and I set out for an even more extended visit to our missionaries in Japan, Korea, Taiwan and Hong Kong.

The air flight from Toronto to Tokyo was a memorable experience. We chased the sun all the way. Because two typhoons occupied our scheduled flying path, we had to lengthen our journey by going north via Anchorage, Alaska. We crossed the International dateline and arrived in Tokyo at 5:00 P.M. local time on the day after we left Toronto—having been in daylight all the time.

We were, however, not finished with the typhoons. At the end of our first day in Tokyo we went to bed with warnings that the storm would strike Tokyo at 9:00 P.M. At the appointed time it came in all its fury. But some time after midnight the wild roar of the winds was augmented by an ominous rumbling. It did not take us long to realize

Moderatorial travels: on a visit to Paddy Sellars,
then on a mission field in Goose Bay.
I made it to Labrador here at Mushcat Falls.

that the predicted typhoon had teamed up with an unpredicted earthquake. We had four more shakes before morning. Despite everything, when morning came we learned that while heavy damage had been done in other areas, our part of the city escaped relatively free.

We wondered if starting with a cyclone and an earthquake were an omen.

We went from Toyko to Seoul, Korea for twelve exciting and instructive days in that remarkable land. Our hosts there were the Rev. and Mrs. Donald Irwin, but the whole company of Canadian missionaries joined in to keep us in a continual party. We saw there the earlier stages of the industrial enterprise that was soon going to startle the world. We saw also some desperate poverty—a local pastor, for example, living on a salary of eight dollars a month plus what he could make from his little flock of goats. We learned, as we were to do later in Japan, the enormous importance of gaining entrance to the few good universities and the incredible pressure parents put on their children to strain for high marks. High school and university years were not years of pleasure, anywhere we went.

Before we left Korea, I was the recipient in Seoul of an honour which made me feel that something was not in proper balance. At an elaborate ceremony in City Hall I was presented by the Mayor with honourary citizenship, given the symbolic "Key to the City," and a beautifully decorated scroll in Korean and English commemorating the event. In the presence of our missionaries I felt a bit uneasy. I had done nothing for Korea. They and their predecessors had. Yet as testimony of Korea's gratitude for *their* great service, the honour was given to me because I held office. That seemed uncomfortably symbolic of too much of our public life.

We went to Hong Kong—a place defying description. There the Rev. and Mrs. Walton Tonge acted an interpreters for us of the difference between our world in Canada and theirs in that strange splinter of China. Two other missionaries, Rev. Alfred Day and Miss Jean Winsor—a distant cousin of mine—gave competent direction to our crowded days. The whole company of our missionaries seemed to merge into one happy welcoming committee. We found again how much more the travellor can learn with informed briefings than is possible by wandering about as a tourist.

From Hong Kong we jumped to Taiwan where Dr. and Mrs. Bruce Copland and Ruth MacLeod briefed us well on the long association of Taiwan with the church in Canada. Mrs. Copland later wrote a fascinating book, *Moon Cakes and Maple Sugar,* telling of her life in China and in the beautiful island of Formosa, now Taiwan.

Our longest visit was back to Japan. There we had a substantial group of specialized workers, some of whom were second generation missionaries and spoke Japanese fluently. Others with unusual talent, like Heinz Guenther, picked up the language quickly. To many, though, the Japanese language was an impenetrable barrier.

It must be remembered that for many years the United Church of Canada has sent missionaries only in response to requests, and only to work under the authority of the local church. All of the missionaries we visited were people with special training doing work for which the church had invited them. In Japan a substantial number of the missionaries were engaged in some form of teaching, though Case Moerman from Manitoba was a specialist in agriculture.

In Japan we owed so much to so many, that it would be hardly fair to do less than to make a roll call of them all, including our Japanese hosts and friends. As I cannot in this record do that, I can only mention that the Ian MacLeods, the Len Keighleys, the Heinz Guenthers and the Howard Normans masterminded events that gave us an ex-

200

in the intangibles of the soul
we had acquired
the wealth of ages

citing introduction to Japanese culture. Once more, we had the enormous advantage of informed briefing.

When our visit was ended, the two tours having taken us on more than 20,000 miles of travel, we headed east for Hawaii for a few days with no duties, no appointments and no speeches, just a time to rest and soak in the sun. Then we went on to Los Angeles to visit Esther's father, then in his nineties, and other members of her family.

Finally we headed east on our last lap toward home, which we greeted with joy on the first of a Canadian November. Chronologically we were only two months older than when we left, but in the intangibles of the soul we had acquired the wealth of ages.

I shall mention just one more of my moderatorial journeys—in some ways the most memorable of all: my attendance in Edinburgh at the General Assembly of the Church of Scotland.

The United Church of Canada since its founding in 1925 has received from the Scottish Presbyterians an important stream of members and clergy. The two churches have kept in close and cordial relationship. When the schedule permits, the United Church Moderator usually attends the Scottish Assembly as a fraternal delegate. This I did in May, 1965.

The Scottish General Assembly is unique. As a Protestant performance, its colour, its contrasts, its anomalies and its excellencies have nothing in the world remotely their match. As fraternal delegate from more lack-lustre courts across the sea, I could hardly fail to find something delightfully incongruous when, in the home of allegedly austere Presbyterianism, the opening of the highest church court was announced in the newspaper with a six-column photograph of the Lord High Commissioner and his suite at the Palace of Holyroodhouse, twenty-two of them in a rich variety of formal dress: Maids of Honour, Lady in Waiting, Purse-bearer, Superintendent of the Palace, Master of the Horse (this particular functionary having a somewhat uncertain standing in religious convocations) and, oh yes, somewhere among the others, a chaplain.

With this introduction I was the more impressed to be delivered a scroll bearing a Royal Coat of Arms informing me that the Purse-Bearer had been commanded by the Lord High Commissioner and Lady Birsay to invite me to dinner in the Palace of Holyroodhouse, and that I was to wear Evening or Highland Dress with Decorations. (Fortunately my clerical garb, especially with moderatorial purple, got me over this last hurdle.)

At that dinner I could not help noting that there were more dress kilts than clerical collars, and enough ceremonial swords for a regimental reunion.

All my life I have had an affinity for odd coincidences. Going to that dinner, I had one of the nicest. As I was leaving my hotel and entering the elevator, a man and woman in full formal dress were already there. They were about forty; she was as lovely as any Scottish lassie for whom Burns would write poems. I guessed that they too might be going to the palace, but in Scotland in such circumstances I was unsure whether or not to speak first. Customs differ. (As I once heard Leonard Brockington say, "In Britain, I do not know whether I should lift my hat to a lady in an elevator, or elevate my hat to a lady in a lift.")

This time there was no problem. They guessed that I was going to the dinner and they spoke first. They introduced themselves, Lord and Lady Murray from their parish in the North of Scotland where Lord Murray was an elder. They invited me to come in their cab to the palace.

Later when I entered the huge dining hall and went to find my place card (again with its royal coat of arms) I saw with it a second card saying, "The Right Rev. E.M. Howse will escort Lady Murray to dinner." I have that card still.

For that evening I had won the jackpot. Nobody had a pleasanter companion nor one easier to talk to.

Other social events included a second visit to Holyrood Palace for a Garden Party. But, for all the pomp and circumstance, the Assembly itself, day by day, kept its proceedings on a level of dignity and of excellence that need not take second place to any democratic ecclesiastical court in any church anywhere in the world. I attended the sessions regularly and followed the arguments with lively interest. The most significant decision made that year was to vote—at long last—approval of women elders in the Kirk.

As to women ministers, that contentious question was postponed for further reflection.

*Dr. George Pidgeon, the first Moderator of the United Church
of Canada and former pastor of Bloor Street Church,
with his successor as minister, and with a member of the church,
Dr. Robert McClure, both also Moderators.
Later there was a fourth Moderator from Bloor street, my successor,
the Rev. Bruce McLeod.*

At one evening session, I brought to the Assembly the greetings of
the United Church of Canada, and spoke briefly about the rich
heritage both our churches traced to the same roots.

It was thirty-one years since as an overseas student I had sat in the
same hall, and heard the address given by the then Lord High Commissioner, our Canadian Governor General to be, John Buchan.

The 22nd General Council of the United Church which would elect
the next Moderator was to meet in September, 1966, in Waterloo,
Ontario. At that time I would be out of office.

Curiously enough, my last days brought from some undisclosed
source a spasm of newspaper speculation that I might "shatter

church precedent" by being re-nominated and elected for a second term. I knew nothing of this. I was in London, England, attending meetings of the World Methodist Federation, of which the United Church of Canada is a member. I learned of it only when I got a call from a Toronto reporter saying that the report of my probable re-election had been published and asking me if I intended to be a candidate for a second term.

Later I learned that both the *Globe and Mail* and the *Telegram* had run stories of this proposal.

The *Globe,* describing me as "one of the most liberal and outspoken (Moderators) of the church's history" attributed its information to "a high-ranking United Church spokesman." The *Telegram*, listing my Moderatorship as "one of the most colourful, controversial and outspoken in the history of the church," said that "a number of ministers here say he has strong support for re-election."

When the reporter got me on the phone, however, the idea was new to me. I explained that whatever might be the legal possibilities I had been for two years largely away from my congregation and that I could not possibly stand for re-election. I said also that I did not think that I had "the ghost of a chance" of being re-elected.

So the issue died at birth. Who raised it and leaked it to the newspapers I have never had the slightest idea.

Only a few days after that telephone call, I was back in Canada and in Waterloo to preside over the opening of the 22nd General Council. I gave the Moderatorial address, and then called for the election. An old friend of mine, Dr. Wilfred Lockhart, President of the University of Winnipeg, gained the majority vote. I passed the stole of office on to him and brought to a close two unforgettable years.

It was easier to get rid of the stole than to get rid of the duties. Each Moderator is required for the term of his successor to remain on the Executive and Sub-executive; and as may be needed, to act as deputy for the Moderator. So I could not quite cut the strings of office until 1968.

Indian Summer

*leaving the pulpit
and picking up the pen*

By 1968, I was 66 years of age, and I realized that the time had come when I should make plans for retirement. In Bloor Street the urgency was perhaps less than it might have been in some other congregations. Bloor Street had a tradition of keeping its ministers to the end; and Bloor Street ministers traditionally had staying power. Dr. Wallace, the founding minister, had stayed for thirty years. When I arrived, both Dr. Pidgeon and Dr. Wallace, (the latter well on in his nineties) who together had been ministers of the church for sixty-three years, were on hand to meet me. My conclusion was, I said, that when a minister was called to Bloor Street Church there was simply no point in going to heaven.

I retired in June 1970, just a few weeks from my 68th birthday. I was coming up to the 50th anniversary of the year, 1921, when I first went as an eighteen year old Methodist probationer to the little fishing outport of Burgeo.

The Bloor Street congregation had an evening to honour Esther ~~Howse~~ and me. That farewell party, presented I am sure under the direction of my assistant, David Allan, was an event even among farewells.

At the start, they brought me up the centre aisle of Bloor Street Church in a boat, one of the parting gifts. From there on it was a time of hilarity. Tributes that were kindly roasts were interspersed with verses adapted to the pattern of Gilbert and stolen from tunes of Sullivan. The verses were composed by Frances Russell, a long time Bloor Street member and a writer of great talent. "The Modern Moderator-O" was set to the Major-General's song in *HMS Pinafore;* and another song, a life history, entitled "The Importance of Being Er-

he dismissed it
with just one adjective—
"awful"

nest" was set to the air "Squarin' up time."

As the rollicking program went on, never did a congregation seem happier in saying goodbye to its minister. However, mingled with the laughter, the meeting managed to commemorate my parting with praise that was an overflow of good will. At the close, thrown on a large screen at the front of the church, the following was the text of the official tribute:

The Very Rev. Ernest Marshall Howse

From 1948 to 1970 you have been our minister
In all things you have been the model
of Christian life and ministry.
By you we have been made richer.
By you the sum of this earth's goodness has increased.

You have rejoiced and suffered with us.
You have accepted us and struggled with us.
You have reminded us of the church
and the world outside our parochial selves.
You have given us long perspectives.

"He was a scholar and a ripe and good one;
Exceeding wise; fair-spoken and persuading;
Lofty and sour (he seemed) to them that loved him not;
But to those men that sought him—sweet as summer."

W. Shakespeare
Henry VIII

We thank you, Dr. Howse!

In return what more could we say than, "Thank you, friends of Bloor Street."

My retirement from the pastorate did not mean that I would have nothing to do. I had undertaken to write for the *Toronto Star* a weekly column for its Saturday Religion page.

Writing for a newspaper, even writing a regular column, was for me not a new venture.

During my years in the pastorate I had written for a variety of papers and periodicals, dozens of book reviews. I had found the writing of reviews a convenient and inexpensive way of augmenting my library. Also, while I was in Winnipeg I wrote quite a number of pieces, including editorials, for the Winnipeg *Free Press*. In 1957 I had begun to write a regular column for that paper.

This was after I had left Winnipeg. I had returned for a brief visit to take anniversary services at Knox Church. During the weekend I was talking to Victor Sifton, editor and publisher of the *Free Press,* and he mentioned his dissatisfaction with what was then called the "Church Page." He dismissed it in just one adjective—"Awful." He invited me to write a regular column on topics I would be free to choose. He said, "I want something on the church page fit to go on the editorial page."

As soon as I returned to Toronto, I began to write that column, and before long, with the friendly co-operation of the *Free Press,* I began to self-syndicate it to about half a dozen Canadian newspapers ranging geographically from the Ottawa *Citizen* to the Victoria *Colonist*. I wrote that column for over seven years, more than four hundred articles. One of them recorded the death of Victor Sifton.

When I became Moderator I had to give up the weekly column. But the Toronto *Telegram* immediately invited me to write a monthly column. As this would mean that I would always have a reserve gateway to the public, I agreed. The *Telegram* had already sent me as special correspondent to the New Delhi Assembly of the World Council of Churches, and would later send me to Uppsala.

My *Free Press* columns, though they had come to an end, had some further circulation when the Ryerson Press made a selection of fifty of them and published the miscellany in a book entitled, *People and Provocations.*

My Toronto *Star* columns, before I had written the first one, brought me an unexpected and extraordinary bonus. Just as I was arranging for the column with Mr. Beland Honderich, publisher of the *Star,* I received an invitation to attend in Kyoto, Japan, a remarkable convocation, one of a sort never before attempted.

What made this different from any previous conference in history was that it was planned as a meeting of representatives of *all* the important religions of the world: Buddhists, Hindus, Christians, Jews, Sihks, Jains, Confucians, and a number of others.

An international group of many faiths had already put in an enormous amount of preparation over several years. Participants who would give the main addresses constituted a roster of world celebrities: Sir Zafrulla Khan, President of the International Court of Justice; Dr. Hideki Yukawav, Nobel prize winner; Archbishop Helder Camara of Brazil; and so on. Altogether there would be 210 delegates chosen from ten religions and 39 countries. Three invitations went to Canada; to Roman Catholic Bishop Remi de Roo of British Columbia; to Rabbi Gunther Plaut, of Toronto, and to me. How I happened to be chosen, I have no idea. I presume that it was because I had already been in so many inter-faith adventures.

When I showed Mr. Honderich the documents and my invitation he immediately said that the *Star* would send me there, to report the proceedings.

So it came about that my first autumn free of pastoral responsibilities was transformed into a time of extraordinary interest. Early in October, Esther and I set out for Kyoto and the Conference.

The Conference itself was an extraordinary affair. Kyoto is a city of an immemorial past, for a thousand years (until recent times) the capital of Japan, and a shrine alike of Japanese history and Buddhist faith. Yet we met in a magnificent new building designed for the multilingual conferences sponsored by the United Nations. It seemed to be a symbol. Every day our strangely assorted company, in debates and conversations, came at times to the edge of an infinite chasm dividing the old from the new. Yet in its entirety the conference was a demonstration that the world in our times had changed. It reflected a deep underlying desire of all peoples of all faiths for peace, and even, in that desire, a willingness to sit down together as equals and as members of one human family, to work together for the good of all.

What was amazing was not so much that the meeting was called together but that it stayed together. At the end it drafted a message to speak to the world. One paragraph sets the tone:

> "To one and all, beginning with ourselves, we say that the point of departure for any serious effort in the human enterprise ... is a solemn acceptance of the fact that (we) are now united in one destiny. We live or die together .... We pledge ourselves to warn the nations whose citizens we are that the

effort to achieve and maintain military power is the road to disaster.''

The World Council on Religion for Peace, constituted in Kyoto that October in 1970, is now one of the permanent religious institutions of the world. I was pleased and honoured to crown all my years in interfaith enterprises by being a founding member of so significant a movement in world religion.

The Kyoto meeting was not the last overseas conference which I was able to attend. I had one more, the fifth Assembly of the World Council of Churches, held in Nairobi, Kenya in the fall of 1975. As I have already mentioned, I was there as special correspondent of the Toronto *Star,* not to report directly but to keep informed of world issues.

However, while I did not attend any more international gatherings, I continued writing my weekly column for the *Star* and that kept me with a lively interest in all the issues of human life.

On the city of Toronto's Civic Honors Day, 1980,
then Mayor John Sewell presented me with an
Award of Merit and Medallion.

Chapter 19:

The Touch of Winter

*life is more
than death can explain*

As the years went on I began to wonder how much longer I should keep on writing the *Star* column. Two dates for possible termination flickered occasionally in my mind: 1980, ten years after I began; 1982, when I myself should come to my 80th birthday.

As it happened, I did not reach either of these dates. In January, 1979, an unexpected intrusion of fate abruptly wrote "30" to all my efforts.

Because I had prepared for a winter holiday, I had a number of pieces already written to fill in for the next two months. So, for a brief time, the columns kept coming; but I was not writing.

I had only one more column to write. It was not just a regular column. It appeared as a feature in the Sunday *Star* on Easter Sunday, April 15, 1979. Perhaps to excerpt that column here will be the best way to tell the story.

> A few weeks ago it seemed to me a fateful certainty that Easter, 1979, would be my last alive.
>
> The truth struck like a thunderclap in winter. As a routine matter I had taken a physical examination. Although in my 77th year, I had not an ache nor a pain, nor any glimmer of intimation that I was not as well as I had been five years before....
>
> With shock and disbelief I learned that I had an abdominal growth, so far unobtrusive but already extensive, and looking suspiciously like a cancerous extension of the pancreas. (I am writing as a layman; a doctor would report it differently.)
>
> That gloom deepened when a long series of sophisti-

cated hospital tests ... all tended to confirm the diagnosis.

Then came the complications. Believe it or not, despite my age, I contracted what seemed to be a variety of old-fashioned childhood whooping-cough.

Certainly, the coughs were bone-shaking; and the whoops would have served for a Newfoundland fog-alarm.

Partly for this reason, the exploratory operation for biopsy and analysis was postponed for 10 days. And for that reprieve I was sent back home, still inwardly feeling —apart from the nuisance of the cough—a tough old-timer, sound in wind and limb.

But by this time I wanted to know the score. Because I had kept active, even after retirement, I had never got around to winding up my affairs, arranging my papers, publications, writings; deciding what should go to archives and what to family history; apportioning my trivia to the members of my family—nor even settling my finances, the disposition of which might have shaken the whole economy of Canada.

The time came when I told my surgeon that in my new situation I wanted to know the plain truth—no syrup. I had work to do. I wanted to have some realistic idea of my time span.

The young doctor sat silently on the bed, and at last spoke quietly. He emphasized that there was no certainty, and as yet no confirmation from surgical examination. But he did not blur the fact that, so far, the presumptive evidence suggested a life expectancy of perhaps six months—maybe doubled, maybe halved.

For that, I give the doctor credit. If there comes another such moment I want the same honesty. If death is lingering in the shadows, I prefer to know what term of days I may still reasonably expect to command.

The delay in operation released me to an unexpected interlude of activity. At home, morning, noon and night, I went through files and cabinets and dusty cartons stuffed with notes of research from times and causes now far behind....

But, above all, the ten days transiently spent at home, augmented by my better days in the hospital, became the grand-daddy of all family reunions.

The two grandparents and four grandchildren, on Boxing Day, 1981

The old family home, lately muting the quiet footsteps of my wife and myself, became the foyer for national traffic.

My own generation of household kin, children with their mates and grandchildren from Toronto, Kingston, and Calgary strolled in the door as though from across the street. And from Florida, and places elsewhere, others, linked by home and blood, picked up telephones and began to give Mother Bell her greatest boost in revenues since she went to Saudi Arabia.

For those who could crowd in a stolen hour or overnight we had some rollicking family meals with their intervals of joy when we all savored the good of life.

The light could not be wholly free from the peripheral shadow of death. But death has seldom been more properly put in its place. We were still celebrating life.

Yet every human being lives at last in an infinity of solitude. No mortal mind ever quite meets another.

Around our chattering board I could not tell from what brief silence some voiceless thought at times was shrieking outrage in the primal scream of protest against the last enemy of us all.

I knew only that, as I sat at the head of that crowded

213

family table and shared in its bright vivacity, I could be stabbed by my own searing pain to think that come, say Christmas, they would be there again, rightly reinforced with their own springs of inward joy; but I would not be there. For me a veil of darkness—the final darkness, to be lifted nevermore.

I reflected how different the reality for the survivor and for the one who dies. The survivor loses one. He who goes down to death loses all. His farewell is the last salute to eternity.

Yet what more could I desire? I can glean no solace from the notion that somewhere beyond the dissolution of my physical being I can somehow remain an unembodied nothing.

Our frail humanity must come sometime to say, "Goodbye," and that last break, for those who die and those who wait a while shreds that transient bundle of life without which existence by itself lacks worth and meaning.

I am a part of all mankind. But not as I am part of my own family. I never knew my grandparents. They had

Making imaginary music, with Andrew, in 1980.

214

died before I was born. I do know the inexpressible debt I owe to the two remarkable individuals who were my father and mother. I know my children and my grandchildren. I am a part of their life, as they are a part of mine.

But my grandchildren will have grandchildren who will have grandchildren. How small a part their lives of mine!

I am not in any way tempted by the notion that I as an individual, now with body and mind, will keep on, generation after generation, infinity after infinity, forever remaining me, never to escape the recurring decimal of my former being.

Should it then be strange that, while I can no longer think of eternal life as simply an infinite extension of individual identity, I can find real meaning in the Easter affirmation that life is greater than death, and hear the glory of Easter music coming to us as the bending of heaven to earth?

Not at all! Always truth comes to us hidden in myth. We can say nothing worth saying; we can stretch for no meaning that exalts our being, save as we pass from the Fact to the Ideal.

I do not need the literal crudity that a battered human body could ascend through the dark infinities of a physical universe. The universe has far more than that to tell me that the things which are not seen are eternal.

Did not Canon Streeter say that the figure of a man hanging on a cross for the sake of an ideal was the inmost mystery of creative power?

It is that mystery, shining through all darkness, that lifts us again to tiptoe in the Hallelujah Chorus. It says more than we can explain; it explains more than we can say.

My diagnosis, which set this Easter as my last, has now been changed. But no matter. Whenever it may be that I hear for the last time the last syllable of ''The Lord God Omnipotent Reigneth'' I will know that what that exultant Hallelujah is saying about life will be more than all the rest of recorded speech can explain about death.

215

The old man supervises rebuilding another dock,
this time at our present cottage on Lake of Bays, in Muskoka.
The other workers are our son George, left,
and son-in-law Ray Dyer.

Chapter 20

Roses in December

*God has given us
memory*

When I wrote that piece the apparent certainty of death had been converted into a reasonable hope for remission. I was not yet out of the woods. I had a total of three abdominal operations, months of chemotherapy, the side effects of which suggested a change to radiation, the side effects of which gave me shingles and Bell's Palsy, the side effects of which have left me with minor paralysis of one cheek. For variety, I had a few days of pneumonia. But really, in it all, nothing too bad. My discomfort from chemotherapy was negligible, far less than that of many who undergo the treatment.

And I emerged from it all with the cancer apparently brought to a full halt, so that for almost two years I have not been taking any medication whatever.

I am one of the fortunate. I have no idea how long the remission may continue; but every day it lasts makes it less likely to return at all.

Meanwhile, like all human beings, I am subject to the erosion of the years, and at my age I keenly hear "Time's winged chariot hurrying near." Cancer or not, I know that there is no armor against fate and no final remission of death.

I have had a good day. I have few desires left for myself. My concerns are for others, but centered in my children and grandchildren.

The deepest satisfaction of my years, and the last comfort that will come to my conscious thought, are the joys of knowing that my three children, Margery, David and George, are playing a worthy part in the generation that will survive when mine is gone, and that their children in turn give promise of passing on from generation to generation the best things I have hoped to be and never quite succeeded in being. And therewith I can take my final rest.

I am happy also that Margery's husband and David's wife have brought so much of worth into the family heritage. David's wife, Ena Robbins, a Newfoundland girl hitherto unmentioned, has been a nurse, a head nurse (at the Hospital for Sick Children in Toronto), and is at the time of writing a teacher of nurses at Queen's University—a person of many gifts and graces.

As I come to the close of all that I have here attempted to review, I reflect with wonder on the mysterious kaleidoscope of events which has marked the passage of my years.

In the variegated fabric of my experience, perhaps there is one thread that runs with a distinctive tint throughout the whole. Partly by chance, because I happened to be at the right place at the right time, partly by my own deep concern, I have had one singular measure of good fortune.

From that distant day when I first saw in Burin harbour that un-suspected harbinger of radical change, an internal combustion engine, to all those later times when I have been privileged to attend some new enterprise in human relations, I have witnessed and some-times shared in significant ventures of a world in transition. I have been involved at the forward edge in the most important ventures of this century in the cultivation of human brotherhood.

In Beverly Hills and later in Winnipeg I was with the pioneer groups which seriously began the cultivation of better relations bet-ween Christians and Jews. In the successive Assemblies of the World Council of Churches I saw the birth of new harmonies within Christian denominations. In the Middle East I shared in the first ten-tative contact where leaders of Christians and Muslims reached out hands to each other across the years of hate. And in Japan I was one of the first company bringing together, in a common search for world peace, representatives of all the great religions of our human kind. In a minor key I can say like Caesar: All of this I saw, and part of this I was.

All of this, too, has been part of these eventful years since I was born in 1902. True, they have also been years of dreadful storm and stress: The first World War; the great Depression; the second World War; the birth of the atomic bomb; the dreadful spread of vaster and vaster agony for countless millions of our fellow human beings. Misery *in excelsis*.

Yet even in that murk many lights have shone, and I am warmed with an inner glow as I remember the defiant phrase of St. John that light is still shining and the darkness has not been able to put it out.